Goodbye Ju~~
Hello Cruel V

Louie Anderson

Louie Anderson's first book, the story in letters of his relationship with his alcoholic father, has already become a self-help classic. Now, for the enormous audience that catapulted *Dear Dad* onto national bestseller lists, the celebrated comedian has something to say about Mom and too much apple pie...nurturing and nourishment...eating, addiction, and self-esteem. An intimate chronicle of Anderson's physical and psychological battle to lose weight and learn how to relate to his drug of choice—food—*Goodbye Jumbo* is a bittersweet, relentlessly honest story told with Louie's special, insightful brand of humor.

Broader in scope than *Dear Dad*, dealing with one of today's most prevalent and baffling diseases, confronting issues of family and self-worth that all readers can relate to, here is the new blockbuster of recovery from a man with a mission—and the humor to deliver it with no medicinal aftertaste.

Louie Anderson, the comedian and bestselling author of *Dear Dad*, grew up in St. Paul, Minnesota. A frequent guest on "Late Night with David Letterman," "The Tonight Show," and "Arsenio Hall," he has starred in four HBO and Showtime specials.

Summer 1993
publication
ISBN 0-670-83766-0

VIKING

GOODBYE JUMBO
HELLO CRUEL WORLD

ALSO BY LOUIE ANDERSON

Dear Dad

LOUIE
ANDERSON

VIKING

GOODBYE JUMBO

CRUEL WORLD HELLO

This book is dedicated to myself . . .
and Jumbo the elephant

I swear the earth shall surely be complete to him or
   her who shall be complete,
The earth remains jagged and broken only to him
   or her who remains jagged and broken.

—Walt Whitman

· · · · ·

If you heal the inside, the outside will heal itself.

—Me

Acknowledgments

I like to think of this book as the hot skinny on being fat. Despite what you have heard about obesity, despite what you are going to read on the following pages about being too big for your britches, it has not been all bad.

In many ways, being fat saved my life. I honestly believe that. Although the extra weight made me different—physically and mentally—from everybody else, it also proved a friend. An unfailing friend. It gave me a place to hide. It was a buffer between me and the world. It was protection against having to reveal what was inside.

GOODBYE JUMBO

xii   From deep within that fortress of south-of-the-border overhang, I felt safe from the gusting arctic cold that greets you every day when you're different.

When you're different, you have two choices. You can either deny everything and spend a lifetime on the run. Or you can spend every day searching for truth, trying to make the best of a world overflowing with cruelty, lies, anger, distress, hate, confusion, and uncertainty.

It's taken me a while, but I made my choice.

To that end I have to thank Jim Gitar, the only person over this long haul who has always been honest with me.

Believe me, writing this book has been a haul, considering all the baggage I forced myself to deal with. Many times I felt as if I had taken on too much, that I was being too honest with both you, the reader, and myself.

I know a lot of what I have to say is going to be unsettling to a few people, especially members of my family. But I decided that I had to confront the fears of my family, the legacy that has bound all of us Andersons. And I had to follow my heart.

I didn't want to publish this book. When I finished, I wanted to burn the manuscript. But from the many thousands of letters I've received since the publication of my first book, *Dear Dad*, I feel as if I started, or in some cases deepened, a relationship with a lot of people who don't need any more disappointments in their lives. This book should bring all of us up to date.

I think there's one more book in me, one more about myself. Time will tell, though.

For now, I'm sick of writing about me, me, me.

As with *Dear Dad*, I had help from my friend Todd Gold.

I gave him a lot of stuff, and he helped to create what you see here. Without him, I would never have been able to write this, let alone finish it. So thank you, Todd.

Also, thanks to you.

xiii

H E L L O   C R U E L   W O R L D

Contents

Preface:
Welcome to the Jungle

A   h, the warmth of the water. The well of the past. A murky depth that makes me smile inside. It's the memories.

Memories.

Of what?

The great gray cloud. Of skin? Of dust? Of what? What am I remembering that fills me with the comfort of infancy?

Then it slips away. Out of my grasp. Like a bar of . . .

· · · · ·

GOODBYE JUMBO

"Where the hell's the soap?" I said.

Oh well.

Pulling myself out of the warm, sudsy bath water, I caught a glimpse of myself in the partially fogged mirror. Was this bathroom minuscule or was I just big? What struck me most was my size. I could see only small parts of myself in the few clear spots on the full-length mirror. But even those parts of my body were large.

I shifted my position. My weight followed. An arm. An elbow. A thigh. Even my toes were big.

Geez.

As the water dripped off my body, I stared dumbstruck at the mirror. Make that awestruck.

I recognized a familiar sight looking right back at me. And it wasn't my reflection.

Where had I seen that fellow? Where?

Then it hit me. Of course.

It was on one of those nature shows that always play on the Arts and Entertainment channel. A documentary on elephants. I looked just like one of those gray-flannel fellows, one of those over-padded pachyderms, great and lumbering, big and slow and hulking and . . .

Fat.

Okay. There. I said it.

Fat.

• • • • •

I looked just like one of those elephants slowly trudging up out of the river.

Using my towel, I wiped the mirror clear and studied my reflection with the detached look of, first a scientist, then a psychologist, and then a comedian. My skin seemed to thicken, harden. My head dropped, and my shoulders rose and my arms dangled toward the floor, giving in to the pull of gravity.

I felt sort of wobbly and unsteady. All of a sudden my two big club feet didn't seem enough to keep me balanced. Fighting the urge to get down on all fours, I drifted into a gray cloud of confusion and wondered aloud, "Well, Louie, maybe you would've been better off if you'd been born an . . ."

• • • • •

An elephant.
There. I said it.
Elephant.

• • • • •

Enough already! Pulling on my big red robe, I hurried out of the bathroom and away from my reflection. In the red bathrobe, I looked like a circus elephant. I went straight to the hotel suite's well-stocked kitchen, looking for something to eat. I was starved.

Along the way, I thought I heard a calliope playing Big Top music. Scanning the counters, I definitely heard a voice barking, "Hurry! Hurry! Hurry!"

Then I saw them.
Doughnuts.
Bingo.

I bit into a vanilla one large enough to double as an elephant's wedding ring.

My brain and stomach sent urgent messages to each other via my tastebuds. Sugar! Butter! Frosting! Sugar! Butter! **xix**

H E L L O   C R U E L   W O R L D

GOODBYE JUMBO

Frosting! Then: sugar, butter, frosting. Sugar, butter, frosting. And then it was all one big, delicious, tummy-warming taste sensation that sparked a chemical reaction akin to a mother's tender hug. Sugarbutterfrosting! Sugarbutterfrosting!

Ah!

• • • • •

As the thin layer of sweet gooey white icing and lighter-than-air dough melted on my tongue, all the thoughts that had come before melted, too. The jungle. The circus. The music. And the image of me as an elephant.

I spotted my reflection on the side of the toaster oven, and now I looked like a younger Orson Welles or an extremely overweight Jack Nicholson. I finished the doughnut and said out loud, "Now that's more like it."

• • • • •

There was a digital clock on the microwave oven. It was a quarter to eight. In fifteen minutes or thereabouts, I was supposed to amble onstage and do my act. I wondered where the time had gone.

Grabbing a Diet Coke, a couple of extra doughnuts, and then one more for the road—actually, for the walk between the kitchen and the bedroom—I rushed to the closet and pulled on my gray slacks, red shirt, and blue blazer. My performance suit.

I hated those slacks. Some years before, when I'd worn them on "The Tonight Show" with Johnny Carson, one of my many nephews had commented about the pants not fitting as nicely as they could have. He was embarrassed for me, reluctant to tell. But at my urging he stammered that they weren't flattering, that pants should hang and not bind.

What was wrong with those pants?

I watched a tape of that show a hundred times, each viewing more painful than the last. I blamed the pants, telling myself my nephew was right. But pictures don't lie. The problem had to do not with the pants but with my legs. They were fat. Grotesquely fat. Especially in the knee area. Layers of puttylike lard hung over my knees, dripping, flapping, too tired and lazy to stay up around my thighs.

If anything, the pants made my stomach look smaller, drawing attention to my legs.

• • • • •

They were elephant legs.

I couldn't even see my legs unless I looked in a mirror, as I was doing at the moment.

Slowly, as I stared at those thick gray legs, the picture of the elephant returned.

I fought it by biting into another doughnut.

The image grew fuzzy. The elephant disappeared, only to be replaced by Fatty Arbuckle. I scratched, Fatty scratched. I took another bite. Then another, licking my fingers. Fatty waved goodbye. I blinked. There was Jackie Gleason looking back at me.

• • • • •

There was a knock at the door.

"Five minutes, Louie," said the stage assistant who had been sent up to remind me why I was in town.

"Coming," I replied.

xxi

H E L L O   C R U E L   W O R L D

GOODBYE JUMBO

xxii   Grabbing the Diet Coke, I headed for the door and stole a last glance in the mirror. Jackie was still there, watching me. I did one of those over-the-shoulder numbers—a quick look, a smirk, a little shuffle of the feet—all for Jackie's sake, and said, "And away we go."

GOODBYE JUMBO
HELLO CRUEL WORLD

My Life in Fifteen Minutes

1

"**G**ood evening. Sorry I can't stay long. I'm in between meals.

"I went clothes shopping today. To the 'Big Man's' store. Let me ask you this: Why don't they just call it 'Fatsos'?

"What's this one-size-fits-all shit?

"In Minneapolis, we have a store for big women. It's called House of Large Sizes. Have you ever seen the women who go in there? There's a sign on the door that says, 'One woman in store at a time, please.'

"If you think that's mean, let me tell you about myself for **1**

2 a few minutes.

"I've always been fat. When I was born, I weighed sixty pounds. The doctor had to bring a crane to slap my ass.

"They didn't wash me off. The nurse turned a hose on me.

"Most kids' first words are 'Mommy, Daddy.' Not mine. Mine were 'Seconds, please.'

"I was the first kid on the block voted Most Likely to Become a Group.

"In kindergarten, my brothers and sisters used to roll me to school. At nap time, everyone had a cute little rug. I had a braided nine-by-twelve.

"In first grade, the teacher said, 'Louie, stay off the jungle gym.' And as for the teeter-totter, the other kid is still in orbit.

"In second grade, we studied geography. Guess who played the United States? Later to include Canada.

"In third grade, I found paste. You could eat paste. The school had a seven-thousand-dollar budget for paste. And I was the only kid who didn't go to the bathroom that year.

"In junior high, most kids brought their lunch in a brown bag. Mom brought mine in a station wagon.

"Swimming? I was harpooned nine times.

"In high school, we started dating. You know how everyone has a blind date? Well, mine *was* blind. She thought she was going out with twins.

"Even tonight, I was sitting outside on the curb, trying to relax. I got a ticket. Last night, I was towed away.

"I've always had a problem with food. I went to a hypnotist to figure it out. Afterward, I didn't eat any less. But I didn't know it.

"Food just communicates with me. When I walk into a

grocery store, I get a twenty-one-Twinkie salute. The Ho-Hos jump straight into my cart. Pork chops start doing a chorus line. And when I try to get out of the store, the chocolate cake in the bakery department calls me back: 'Hey, Louie, where are you going?'

"I know a lot of you are wondering the same thing: 'Does he know he's that big?' "

Happy New Year

2

People were still applauding as I walked back-stage. I heard several calls for an encore. They wanted more.

I kept walking toward the dressing room, though I under-stood the crowd's need for more: more jokes, more laughter, more time before they had to leave the comfort and closeness we'd created in the auditorium and return home. I knew about the urge for more.

I knew about the desire for excess.

It was New Year's Eve, 1989. I had just finished perform-ing for five thousand people in my hometown, Minneapolis.

4

Which wasn't unusual. Except that it had been a special performance, a nonalcoholic, sober New Year's show. Talk about a hard gig. Everyone in the audience had experienced the tragic underbelly of comedy, weakness, and cruelty.

Me too.

I was a living, breathing, bandaged specimen. My dad drank. My mom stuffed us with food.

But I was different from most of the people in the audience. Not only did I wear the two schizophrenic faces of Pan, I also exploited them. I'd made myself famous doing it. Pretty comfortable in the money department, too. My dad would've called me a goddamned lucky bastard.

Which, I suppose, is a helluva lot better than what he used to call me in the middle of the night:

Lard ass.

• • • • •

After the show, two friends who've known me forever and don't care about my celebrity drove me to the Market BBQ, a rib place that's a close approximation of heaven. The restaurant is a favorite of mine because they serve all the food on a plastic tray. Not a plate. A tray. In case you want to stick your face down in it and snort it up like a pig.

I ordered the biggest rib-and-chicken combo on the menu and a strawberry soda.

Then I snorted until the tray was clean.

• • • • •

I don't do drugs, but I know what it's like to be an addict. You could put a syringe of heroin in front of me and a plate of doughnuts, and I'll choose the doughnuts every time. Every

5

6 single time.

• • • • •

"Dessert?" the waitress asked.

Like the audience I'd just left, I wanted more. Dessert was just the right encore.

"You have to ask?" I answered.

Believe it or not, people often ask, "Do you like to eat?" Oh no, I don't like to eat. Not me.

What do they think? I have a little valve and every day I blow myself up?

She read me the choices: Sundaes. Chocolate cake. German chocolate cake. Lemon cake. Apple pie. Strawberry pie. Raisin pie. Banana cream pie. Tapioca pudding. Bread pudding. Custard.

Then she excused herself because she was forgetting some and wanted to go back to the kitchen to check what they were.

"Don't bother," I said. "The chocolate cake is fine, thanks."

• • • • •

As I entered the hotel, a New Year's party was spilling out into the lobby from the hotel's restaurant. The revelers wore party hats and blew noisemakers. It looked like they were having fun. I passed through unnoticed and went straight to my room. Too exhausted even to watch television, I curled up on the bed in a fetal position, my stomach as full as a newborn baby's. I watched the digital clock on the night table change from 12:00 to 12:01.

Happy New Year!

I rolled over and counted barbecued ribs until morning.

. . . . .

I don't care how big the bed is. Or how soft or hard it is. It's impossible to sleep in a hotel.

Just try to close those curtains. That must be a big joke with those contractors. All of them leave that one-inch slit down the middle. No matter where you lie, the light finds you. Like that picture of Jesus where the eyes follow you.

That's what happened to me. A thin blade of sunlight cut through the otherwise pitch-dark room, slicing my sleeping carcass like a sharp knife going through a hard-boiled egg. My eyes opened a crack, then quickly closed. I realized I'd forgotten to tape the curtains shut.

I rolled over. I pulled up the covers. Then I opened one eye a crack.

Light!

Ouch!

There was no escape. From either the light or my childhood.

I got out of bed and pulled the curtain aside. The first day of the new year was bright and sunny. Once I got my sea legs and adjusted to daylight, I began liking the looks of things. I opened the window and felt the air. It was kind of warm, unusually so for winter in Minnesota. The weather seemed to be offering a ray of hope and optimism.

Best was that the streets were empty, probably the result of everyone sleeping off his hangover. I love driving on days like these. No one's out. I can open the car up. My dad despised being on the road on days like this. No one to yell at. No one to make him feel superior.

8   I thought about driving out to visit my dad's grave, although the last time I'd been there had been very emotional. I'd read him two year's worth of letters I'd written to him that reconciled the relationship we never had. I didn't feel up to a return engagement.

I ordered breakfast from room service instead, my first mistake of the year. Because you can never get the things you really want from room service.

Like orange juice.

"*Au jus?*" shrieks a heavily accented voice, as if you were speaking a foreign language.

"No," I said. "Orange. Juice. It comes in oranges. They grow on trees. The same tree I'm going to hang you from if I have to come down there myself."

• • • • •

Then those room-service guys come into your room looking as if they've just been jumped.

"Where do you want the food?"

"There're two flat surfaces: the table and your head."

I got two bran muffins and a pot of coffee.

• • • • •

People are always trying to get me to eat healthy. I try eating healthy, too. But every time I eat, say, a whole-grain, no-preservatives, all-natural-ingredients, raisin, date, and vitamin-fortified bran muffin, my mouth screams, "Hey, get that outta here!"

• • • • •

There's only one way to eat those muffins. Only one way

to make all those good-for-you ingredients palatable.

Butter.

. . . . .

After slathering the muffins with enough butter to frighten any cardiologist, I glanced through the newspaper. There were the usual stories about senseless homicides and needless homelessness, the same stuff people in every city wake up to. I didn't have to read the stories to know what they said.

Instead I flipped to the arts-and-show-biz section, expecting to find a review of my show and, naturally, bracing myself for the possibility of a bad one. But none appeared. Not a good one or a bad one. Zilch. The reviewers were probably out having a good time with everyone else.

I had thought about flying my mom in for the show from her home in Carson City, Nevada. But I hadn't. And now I felt bad.

It would've been nice to walk outside with her on this slow, warm morning and ask her to fill in some of the blanks I had about my childhood. If those years were a blur to me, though, for my mom—after forty-five years of marriage, eleven children, the stillbirths of five others (her first pregnancy and two sets of twins), and everything else—well, they were probably a blinding snowstorm.

I made a mental note to call her when I got back to L.A. a few days later. I'd prepare a list of questions.

Why I Don't Call

3

After breakfast, I went for a walk to burn off the butter and muffins. Having no planned route, I found myself on Washington Avenue, striding toward the now abandoned Milwaukee Railroad Station, where we used to pick my dad up late at night.

Although she drove to the station and was perfectly capable of getting us back home, my mom turned off the engine and slid over to the passenger seat as soon as she parked. My younger brother Tommy and I sat in the back, fighting to be the first to spot Dad.

10

"Mom, Louie's not looking for Dad," Tommy would whine.

"What's he doing?"

"He's looking at me."

"Am not."

"Are so."

"Baby."

• • • • •

Eventually the train arrived, and my dad appeared among all the others getting off work after a long day of laboring on those very tracks with too little money to show for it. He always walked down the tracks the same way; slowly, head down, eyes scanning the ground.

"You gotta keep your head down," he used to advise us. "You never know when you're going to find some money."

• • • • •

Standing outside the old train station, now quiet and still and empty in the crisp morning air, I watched for the ghosts of another time and listened for echoes of the past. I wondered how it might've been for my family if my dad had been able to keep his head up more often. If he'd been able to look at us more than he did the ground for a bit of loose change.

I wondered if my dad realized that those tracks he worked on were intertwined with our family. I don't think so.

But I later discovered that his father, a prolific inventor who lacked any sort of business sense, actually invented the contraption that allows a train to switch from one track to another.

It made no difference, though. My dad still kept his head **11**

12 down.

. . . . .

I regret I never asked him why. Really pressed for answers that made more than cents.

It's sad how little children know about their parents. Sad how fearful everybody is of talking. Of the truth. The only thing I knew about my dad for absolute certain was that he loved his car.

. . . . .

After two days in town I still hadn't called any of my brothers or sisters. I've got ten of them, although one of my brothers has been homeless for a couple of years and we don't have any idea where he is. I don't think it's an accident that we don't know his whereabouts or that he doesn't have a home.

It's so hard for me to go home.

Why?

That's a good question.

I'm the second youngest of eleven children, and no matter what I accomplish in life, careerwise or for my family, I'll always be in this position, one of the babies. Which means that I'm easily and almost always picked on.

For the most part, my brothers' and sisters' opinion of me hasn't changed for years. In fact, it's probably worsened the more successful I've become. "He used to be nice," they comment when they think I'm out of earshot. "But ever since he got famous, Louie turned into such an asshole."

If I happen to overhear them, or if somebody rats, then they quickly smile and try to soften their remarks by saying,

"Just kidding."

• • • • •

I love my brothers and sisters. But am I close to them?
The answer is: Sometimes.

Sometimes I'm close to some of them, sometimes I'm distant from some of them, and sometimes some of them leave me with no feeling at all.

My feelings about my brothers and sisters change all the time, the way a deck of cards is shuffled by the dealer every couple of hands. And this, I think, is normal for people from families like mine.

When you're from an alcoholic family, feelings are the first things to go. You learn to stuff them away, out of reach. And virtually out of sight. But they're always there, lurking. Like your shadow, they remind you that you're never alone.

• • • • •

"You could help out, Louie," I've heard more than once on a trip home. "Why don't you do a little more? You're such an asshole. If I was in your position, I'd act a lot different than you. But then I'm not surprised. Why should you change?"

Sometimes I'm called nice. Sometimes an asshole. The deck is always being shuffled to suit someone's purpose.

I'm not a dirty fighter. I don't bring up the past. Or use guilt or shame to get my way.

I just tell it like it is.

Which is probably why I don't go home a lot.

• • • • •

13

H E L L O   C R U E L   W O R L D

GOODBYE JUMBO

14 Even cable television was boring, so I lay in bed in my hotel room and examined my hatred.

I hated so many things. So many people. It scared me. But I don't think it's abnormal.

Yet the more I thought about it, the more lists I compiled, the more I heard my mother say, "Louie, we don't hate."

"I do."

"Oh no you don't."

Sometimes I ask audiences if they've ever thought of killing somebody. Usually this is met with an uncomfortable silence, a slight nervous chuckle. Then I say, "You mean you're going to say, 'Oh no, Louie, I've never thought of killing anyone.' Me, every day I have to stop myself from getting a machine gun and opening fire."

The truth is, everybody hates. It's a part of us. I have to work on it often, controlling the emotion, expressing it diplomatically, acknowledging it. My mom laid a lot of shit on me about what's right and wrong, but as I got older I've decided it's okay to hate. It's normal. It's natural.

I wonder, though, if I didn't come to that conclusion a long time ago, when I was a child.

Someone once told me that much of what we know is learned by age two, and then we spend the rest of our life trying to figure it all out. If that's the case, between the ages of one and two, I must have realized that I came from an alcoholic family. I must also have figured out that I was a mistake, that there wasn't enough room in our house or money in my dad's pocket for the other nine kids and two adults, let alone a new baby.

And I must have realized that food was a substitute for the love that a baby craves. I must have figured out that people weren't going to give me the sense of affection and security that a full tummy gave me.

Damn it, I wish I could remember.

•••••

Lying in bed at dinnertime, the TV droning on about some miracle mini waffle iron that cooked everything from party sandwiches to dessert, I realized that I'd spent the past thirty-seven years searching for the love and affection I never knew as a child. That was my problem.

I thought that I'd find it in success. I thought that I'd find it in the spoils of success.

But now that I was spoiled, I was still spinning my wheels.

Nothing was ever enough. No laugh was big enough to dry the tears. No applause was loud enough to replace the hugs I never got. No amount of money could buy what I really wanted. Or needed. No meal could fill the pit in my stomach. No food could satisfy my craving.

•••••

There was love in my stomach, but not in my heart. Why?

•••••

If I realized anything about being fat, it was this:

People don't get fat because they eat too much. They get fat because they need to.

•••••

Elephants eat and eat and eat to store fat for when there is less food available.

15

16   But what was I storing fat for? Had there ever been a time when there wasn't enough to eat? Was there ever going to be such a time in the future?

• • • • •

I picked up the notepad beside the bed and wrote, "Call Mom in the morning and ask why I got fat."

What?

4

Later that night, in my room in the old flour mill turned hotel, I sat opposite a young actor-playwright who had written a show about his father. With the script under his arm, he had come to talk about this territory both of us had in common.

For some reason, I was suffering from a weariness that I couldn't shake. A malaise of the soul. The year was only four days old. But it seemed to me that it had gone on for long enough.

However, I was amused by the playwright, who ate brown **17**

18 rice as he explained his play. Between bites, he lectured me about macrobiotics and . . .

Well, I reached a point where I couldn't absorb any more of what he had to say. His passion and love of work and life was intoxicating, uplifting, the picture of uncontainable energy. It depressed the hell out of me.

Unable to watch him eat any more brown rice, I called room service and ordered dessert. Not because I was hungry but to somehow regain control of a situation that was making me uncomfortable. Several minutes later, a gaunt, reedy man with jet black hair, a deathly white complexion, and delicate white-gloved hands wheeled a cart into the room.

The atmosphere suddenly changed. It was as if his mere presence sucked all the warmth out of the air. The temperature seemed to get as cold as this strange man's icy blue eyes.

"Where would you like me to set this?" he asked.

The playwright and I exchanged looks and communicated the same feeling without saying anything. This guy was creepy. Something strange was happening. We couldn't wait until he left.

"Right there, on the table," I said.

"It's a fine night, isn't it?" He smiled, handing me the bill to sign. "The tip's already included."

As soon as he disappeared, the playwright turned to me and whistled the theme from the "Twilight Zone."

"Who was that?" I asked.

I pulled the cake and ice cream toward me, feeling the need to take a bite. It was the kind of basic, tasty dessert my mother always made. I let the cake and ice cream sit on my tongue for a minute. The flavors mixed. The textures blended. My stomach readied itself. My brain registered that old familiar message, "Ah, sweet comfort."

Finally, I swallowed.

Then I felt relieved enough to resume the conversation. As we talked, the playwright watched me eat. His gaze was intense. I knew what was going on in his head. His thoughts were transparent. Despite his penchant for health food, he wanted to taste my food. He had that look.

I could tell: He was a closet fatty.

"Do you want a bite?" I asked.

"No," he said.

I didn't say it, but I thought, "Liar."

But hey, if he didn't want to admit the truth, fine with me. I understood. There's nothing harder to swallow than the truth. Let him eat his brown rice.

· · · · ·

As the cake and ice cream began to disappear from the plate, I knew it was only a matter of minutes before I'd want to slide into bed, under the covers, and meditate on being full. Which meant I had to get rid of this guy. There was just one problem: I didn't know what to say without being rude.

Suddenly, though, we were interrupted. The telephone rang. One, two, three times.

It was, I thought, probably that eerie guy from room service, wondering if I was ready for him to pick up the empty dishes.

"Aren't you going to answer it?" the playwright asked.

I could see that he was one of those people who didn't understand how anyone could not answer the phone. I didn't see how anyone could.

"My calls are supposed to be held at the desk," I said, and **19**

20 then picked it up.

"What?" I growled.

The operator said it was my brother Jim. He was making an emergency call. I told her to put it through.

"Louie," he said. "It's Mom."

Before he said another word, I knew. It was as if I knew from watching too many movies. I mouthed the next two words as he said them.

"She's dead."

"I'll be right there," I said.

I hung up the phone and looked at the playwright. Looked right through him. Then I turned my gaze toward the cake, thinking of my mom. I picked up the fork and cut off a corner of the dessert and brought it to my mouth, thinking of it as her last bestowal of love for me. That was her way. Unable to give the love she felt, she gave through food.

Now she was gone.

And the cake I put in my mouth suddenly had no taste.

"That was one of my brothers," I said. "He told me that my mom died."

· · · · ·

We didn't say anything more. The playwright just hugged me before leaving.

About fifteen minutes later, I went down to the lobby and told the man at the front desk that I was expecting an important business call, but to tell the caller that I'd had to leave because my mother had just died. Before I finished thanking him, another hotel employee came out from a back room. He saw me and did that familiar double-take people do when they suddenly recognize me as that comedian. He stepped toward me and smiled, "Hey, you're so funny."

"Thanks, man," I said in a muted voice.

The hotel employee sensed that he'd said the wrong thing at the wrong moment. I tried to slough it off and make him feel okay. Why not? I know there isn't a whole lot of difference between comedy and tragedy. Except, of course, when you become aware of the latter.

21

Handling It

5

I sat trancelike in the rental car across from the hotel for at least fifteen minutes. Not a single muscle moved. My body put itself on hold. My mind went into shock.

My mom was a gentle woman who nourished me in her own way. I saw her turning from the front seat of the family Bonneville and reaching around to lock my door.

And then I saw nothing.

My eyes blinked. I don't think I ever felt more alone in a car. In the world. Only the car windshield separated me from the dark void of night. I tried to fool myself. A feebly pleading voice in the back of my brain tried persuading me that I was returning from a night out with friends.

"My mom is dead," I said out loud.

The words came out of me on their own volition. I hadn't planned to say them. Then they lingered for a moment in the heavy air in the car. The sound of them made me shudder, the way I used to in school when someone ran their fingernails down the blackboard. I opened the window to get some fresh air, to let the words escape.

"There. I said it," I uttered aloud.

I'd said it about other people's moms. Even felt sad about their loss. But I'd never thought about my own mother dying. Being dead. The woman who'd grunted and pushed through sixteen births, struggled through life with eleven children and an alcoholic husband who doubled as a twelfth child; the woman who put herself last and the rest of us first.

"She's dead. My mom's dead."

Tears streamed down my face. I had to confront the truth of this horrible matter.

I started the car and drove to my brother Jim's.

· · · · ·

Most elephant families are led by the eldest female, the matriarch, who shoulders the responsibility for the most important part of an elephant's day, eating. That was certainly true in my family.

My mom always started our day with a big breakfast to make up for my dad's drunken rages the previous night. We got hot lunches in place of the new clothes we couldn't afford. After school, there was always a snack awaiting us in place of the many comforts we couldn't afford.

23

HELLO CRUEL WORLD

24   For dinner, she served big steaming bowls of mashed potatoes and meat overflowing on platters too hot to hold. Then we had boats of gravy to cover it all up, almost as if this was my mother's way of hiding the fact that ours wasn't a home as happy as those we saw on television.

There was always dessert. Her homemade chocolate cake with nuts on top made us feel special. And late at night, in front of the TV, we burned french fries to an extra-crispy crunchiness in our deep frier. Pound after pound of sizzling potatoes.

Maybe my mom thought that if we were full enough we wouldn't notice that we lived in the projects, that we shopped at the Salvation Army, that we kids could never have our friends over because we never knew when Dad was going to show up drunk and create a scene that we couldn't explain to the neighbors.

• • • • •

I guess it was her way of saying words that were difficult for her to speak: I love you.

• • • • •

The drive over to Jim's was a blur. I couldn't remember one thing between on-ramp and off-ramp. Except that I worried about facing everyone in my family. They were mad at me. Why? Simple. They resented me for having money, for having become a success, for having left the family fold, and most of all they resented me for trying to reconcile myself with a past all of us shared and make myself healthy.

But I wouldn't hear one word of that tonight and I knew why. There was something more important on the agenda: a funeral. It had to be planned. And then it had to be paid for. Everyone had chipped in when my dad died. But that wasn't going to happen this time. Now, one of the eleven kids had money.

My dad always maintained he didn't care about money. That's because he never had any.

But we had a rich uncle, Uncle Ike, and my dad sure spent a lot of time caring about his money.

"Christ, that bastard could help us out if he wanted to," he used to say.

Later in life, I found out that Uncle Ike *had* helped my dad out. He'd lent him a down payment for a house. But then my dad couldn't pay the mortgage installments and he'd lost it.

My dad never said a kind word about him. Sometimes my family made me feel like my Uncle Ike—you never heard "I like Ike" in our household.

· · · · ·

As I pulled into my brother's driveway, I noticed a van in front of me. It too was just parking. I watched the brake lights flash on and off. My brother Kent and I got out of our vehicles at the same time. We're as different from each other as two people can get, but that didn't matter. Kent, the least likely person in the family to show emotion, walked toward me and gave me a hug.

"I'll never forget a thing you did for Mom," he said.

His show of emotion surprised me. It was uncharacteristic. This was a person who'd spent a lifetime hurting me, his younger brother. Not that I didn't appreciate his sentiment, feel for him. But in families like mine, I knew that things **25**

26 were never as they appeared.

"Thanks," I said. "Let's go inside."

• • • • •

As we went up the walk to Jim's, in my mind's eye I saw myself following a familiar path through the Roosevelt Homes development, the housing project on the east side of St. Paul where I grew up. I entered our house. We called it a house, but it was a duplex. Apartment A. Two stories, four bedrooms, redwood on the outside. In L.A. it'd be worth about three hundred-fifty thousand dollars. But we paid fifty-six dollars a month.

"That doesn't seem like so much," I remember my younger brother Tommy saying to me once when we were kids.

"Shut up," I said, suddenly sounding like my dad. "It's a goddamn fortune."

I padded through the different rooms, stopping in the living room. I saw the mirrored framed picture of the pink flamingos above the sofa. My mom was lying on the couch, watching TV. She looked happy.

I loved it when she lay on her side, her knees bent enough so that I could cuddle up behind her legs. Sometimes I brought a pillow and blanket and burrowed myself in. She'd shift around, making room for both of us, and then once we were arranged comfortably, she'd run her fingers through my hair, making me feel special and cared for.

That was such a safe, secure place.

• • • • •

A baby elephant walks virtually under its mother, nestling as close to her belly as it can. The mother strokes her child with her soft trunk. And somehow they manage not to step on each other's toes.

• • • • •

I never remember my mother yelling at me. Or punishing me. Or being disappointed in me.

She only showed love.

Every morning she greeted me with a smile, and offered me that same smile when I returned home from school, and then again before I went to sleep. Or if she went to sleep first, she gave me a smile and a little peck on the head.

No matter how horrible my dad had been to her that afternoon or the night before.

I never realized how much strength and courage was behind my mom's smile.

• • • • •

I stumbled on the step outside Jim's front door. As I might have predicted, I made an awkward entrance.

Like a herd of elephants, we gathered in Jim's kitchen, but in a break from family tradition no one was eating. We hugged. We stumbled around the house. We bumped into one another, apologizing profusely. The phone rang constantly, aunts, uncles, cousins, nieces, and nephews checking in by the score. And everyone making the same astonished comment: "I can't believe it. How'd it happen?"

The way she would've wanted it, I supposed, though my mom was one of those people so full of life I never imagined her dying. Yet I remember her telling me, "Louie, when I get old, I don't want to suffer. I don't want to lay in a hospital bed being sick and feeble. No, I don't want that for me. I **27**

HELLO CRUEL WORLD

28 want to go like that."

Then she'd snap her fingers.

"Like that."

And that's what she did.

Heart attack.

She'd been in her car. Something happened. She leaned out the window and told her neighbors that her car had died. Talk about prophecies. By the time they reached the passenger side, she was gone.

• • • • •

We waited to hear our matriarch's familiar trumpet. A music only Mom could make.

We waited. And waited. And . . .

• • • • •

Someone had put a picture of Mom on the refrigerator. It was the most recent picture they'd taken of her. Her face bore an unmatched innocence, her eyes radiated hope. She was wearing her favorite green sequined blouse.

"She should be buried in that," I said to no one particular.

"What?"

"She loved that blouse," I said. "She should be buried in it."

"Oh no!" one of my sisters exclaimed.

I wanted to say something but bit my tongue. Any comment, polite, logical, or otherwise, would've been taken wrong. Our leader was gone. The herd sensed the change. They were restless, excited, uncertain, operating on automatic. No one quite knew what to do or what to say or how to act. The confusion was obvious as everyone became absorbed in testing new boundaries, issuing subtle challenges, playing that old family game of "You're an asshole but I'm not going to come out and tell you what I think."

There was something that needed to be said. An issue more immediate than what my mother should wear to her funeral. It had to be dealt with. But I knew no one would bring it up. Not directly, though I knew everyone at Jim's, all my brothers and sisters, had given the issue at least some thought. And then someone blurted it out.

"Well, I don't have any money to pay for it."

"What's that?" someone asked.

"The funeral. Do you know how much they cost?"

At last. It was out in the open. I heard it being talked about from another room and walked directly into the fray. Everyone stared at me. I felt the burn, but had anticipated the heat.

"Don't worry," I said. "I'll take care of it."

No one argued.

"Cookies?" one of my sisters said as she walked into the room. "I have some cookies."

• • • • •

"I'm okay," I told my siblings as we spent the night and the next day bumping into one another. "No, really. I'm okay."

"Good, good, Louie. I'm handling it, too."

• • • • •

The older I get, the more I realize how dishonest adults are. Someone ought to punish them. Of course, most of them spend a pretty fair amount of time punishing themselves. People lie too much—to themselves as much as to one

29

30   another.

Someone ought to slap their hands and say, "It's not okay to lie. It's not okay."

• • • • •

The night air was cool and damp, but the sky's darkness had begun to thin. I sensed the onset of morning. As I left my brother's, trudging down his front path, I looked at my watch. It was five A.M. I didn't feel like going back to the hotel. I didn't feel like going anywhere.

I ended up knocking on my friend Marty's front door. I knew he wouldn't mind. And if he did?

Well, my mom had died. When that happens people let you get away with just about anything.

We started to talk. Then Marty built a fire and I stared into the flames until I lost myself and went into a sort of trance. Marty kept talking, while I half-listened and watched the flames dance above the wood and thought about the last time I'd seen my mom.

Had it been back in Africa?

Yeah, maybe. That time when the entire herd had taken off, scared. The air had been thick with danger. Then something emerged from the bush and began chasing us. It wasn't a hungry lion. No, the herd would've faced that potentially deadly threat by having the big adult elephants surround the young ones.

This danger was greater than any animal. It was foreign to the jungle. Foreign to the natural order of things.

There was an explosion. A flash of lightning.

Then a large female fell to the ground in front of me. Not my mother, but a relative of mine. An aunt.

Frightened, I looked around for my mother. She hurried over to me and stopped suddenly as soon as she saw my injured aunt. Lying on her side, my aunt looked up at us. Earlier that day, she'd played with me in the watering hole, pulling tasty green reeds from the banks and feeding them to me as a treat. Now, she was in pain, bleeding. Dying.

A big tear rolled out of her eye.

• • • • •

There was another explosion. My mother nudged me and began to run. The explosions continued, coming more frequently. My mother ran faster, forgetting to look out for me. I fell behind and then lost sight of her altogether.

I tried running faster, but suddenly there was a vine around my right front leg. I tripped. Struggled to get up. Another vine was tossed around my neck. I was pulled sideways and then onto the ground. Still another vine was put around my hind legs, and then I couldn't move.

Where was my mother?

Without her near me, I felt lost. And scared.

"Get him up and put him in line with the others," I heard a light-skinned man say to some darker-skinned men.

The vines were pulled. My rear was smacked with a stick. I was prodded upright, pushed forward, poked, and jabbed. I noticed cousins and friends beside me. All of us were hungry and tired and frightened.

All of us wanted our mothers.

"Goddamnit," a voice bellowed, "get these ugly animals out of here."

31

HELLO CRUEL WORLD

32

Marty poked the fire with a stick, and the logs broke and crackled and sent up a shower of sparks. I searched my exhausted, traumatized brain for the last time I'd been with my mom.

. . . . .

It was the evening that I filmed my last HBO special, which was also the last time I'd been in Minneapolis. My mom came backstage several minutes before the taping began. The place was hectic, confused, people rushing around. Normally I don't see anyone before a show, but for some reason having my mom backstage seemed to be just the thing I needed to help me focus.

She looked great. Her mood was upbeat, more so than usual, almost as if she was floating several inches off the ground.

"I like that shirt and jacket," she said. "You look good."

We gossiped for a few minutes. And then it was time for her to leave. She got up and I kissed her. She hugged me back. Only she didn't hug me the way she usually did. Her hug this time was longer and stronger, full of meaning that she couldn't convey with words. A lump formed in my throat, and I fought back a tear.

I knew that there was something wonderful about the moment, just as I recognized that there was also something tragic about it, in that it lasted only that one moment.

Later, during the show, I introduced my mom. She waved and got a nice round of applause.

She enjoyed the attention. She often asked me if any of my fans asked about her, knowing full well that they did. Once, I took her with me on "Hollywood Squares," and she stole the show. "What kind of kid was Louie growing up?" John Davidson asked, and without missing a beat she said, "Oh, he always loved to eat."

The crowd roared and she gave me a nudge under the table as if to ask, "How was that?" People who met my mom remembered her. She had a way about her.

33

Together Again

6

"Louie, how about some breakfast?"

Marty snapped me out of my trance. An hour had passed since I'd knocked on his door. The sun was coming up. A pale light crept in through his curtained windows. I was sleepy and hungry, more hungry than sleepy.

"Okay," I said.

Marty wanted to shower first, which was fine with me, since I wanted to check my messages. As I went to get his phone, he flipped on the stereo to an easy-listening station. I dialed my machine in L.A., punched the buttons. No messages. I had been expecting someone to leave word that I was the victim of a not-very-funny practical joke. My mom was still alive.

As I waited for Marty, I sat down in front of his stereo and looked through his records, CDs and tapes. Suddenly my eyes bugged out in pure surprise. Shit. In my hands was an album that was very familiar, an album that I'd grown up with, the album that had proved to my friends that my dad really was famous. It was the Hoagy Carmichael record he'd played on as part of the orchestra.

Actually, when I was growing up we'd never had the album, just the photograph that was now on the cover. But my dad frequently pointed out his place in Carmichael's orchestra and recounted tales of that recording.

"It's a new release," Marty explained. "The record company sent it to me last week. I'm going to review it."

It was unopened, still protected by shrink wrap. I asked if I could play it and then put it on the turntable. I cued the needle directly to the song my dad was featured on. The sound of his trumpet floated out of the speakers. It seemed to me to be isolated from the rest of the orchestra, alone, beautiful, a solo meant to impress.

I listened, and the more I listened the more I began to have the feeling that my mom and dad were together again.

• • • • •

After breakfast, I went back to the hotel and collapsed on the bed for a few hours of restless sleep. Upon waking, I remained burrowed in bed. I didn't want to rise. Or move. Or do anything. Only my fat, round head and the TV remote control were visible from beneath the pile of blankets.

35

H E L L O   C R U E L   W O R L D

36   My mood was ugly. Fighting depression, I found myself mad. Blistering mad. Feeling truly evil. And I couldn't pinpoint why. I took it out on the TV, firing thousands of holes in the screen with the remote.

Bang.

Nothing on that channel.

Bang.

Nothing.

Bang, bang, bang.

Right on up through the Home Shopping Network.

Bangbangbangbangbangbang . . .

Ever notice how fast you get with that clicker?

No.

No, no, nope.

Nonononononononono.

And then, without warning, you come to that get-rich-quick infomercial and wonder, "Hey, what the hell is John Davidson doing in Hawaii?"

Same thing in real life. You're going about your business as always, and then, without warning, it's, "Hey, what do you mean my mom is dead?"

Nothing Fancy

7

With Jim tagging along for support, I went to the funeral home to make the arrangements. I hated the experience. When you're still alive, you owe it to those you love to plan your own funeral. It's always puzzled me that people don't do this. Is it that they want to punish those who survive them, or is it that everyone thinks he's the first person in history who isn't going to die?

The funeral home gave me the creeps. So did the director. He was pale and thin, a stereotype of what a person who works at a funeral parlor should look like. And I resented

38 that he felt sorry for me.

I mean, bullshit. Behind his ashen pallor and sad eyes was a salesman counting his dough. He had paying customers.

My mom had once talked to me about her funeral. Rather, she kind of slipped it into a conversation, sly and casual like.

"Nothing fancy," she said. "I don't want anyone to make a big deal."

Something simple would be more in character for her. But I didn't say anything about that to the funeral director as he gave Jim and me various pitches, "suggestions," he called them, about limousines, types of services, and what wardrobe we wanted. I didn't know what to say.

For once, I didn't have an opinion. In fact, I didn't want any part of it.

So I said, "Yeah, that sounds good. I'll take it."

I mean, he could've been selling me a horse and carriage for all I knew.

"Very good," he said, smiling sympathetically. "But we still have to talk about, well . . ."

"What?"

"The casket."

Picking out a casket is similar to buying a new car, only worse. Seeming as if he could barely contain his sadness, the salesman ushered Jim and me into an eerie area of the show-room. Cool and dimly lit, it was what I imagine eternity to be like. Soft music, say, the Carpenters, wouldn't have been out of place. The caskets were lined up in rows, their lids open, a little white card with the price on it set inside where Mom would lie.

"Look around," the salesman told us.

I expected him to say, "Enjoy." He didn't. I was hopeless,

useless. I stood in one spot, in a daze.

"How about this one?" Jim said, snapping me back to reality.

"Fine," I said.

It was white. Both of us liked it. More important, both of us thought Mom would like it, too.

• • • • •

"I'm sure glad that's over," Jim sighed as we pulled away from the funeral home and sped past the surrounding cemetery, heading toward the big iron gate separating the grounds from the living world. We passed through.

"It's funny," I said, scanning the grave markers.

"What?"

"What Dad always said about cemeteries."

"What's that?"

"That people are dying to get in there," I said, laughing as if it really was funny.

I was exhausted, and my internal clock told me it was time for a nap.

But instead of sleep, I was tortured by the constant pull of the vine around my neck and the periodic sharp, painful, rib-bruising prod of the steel-tipped stick wielded by a stocky, sweaty man with a menacing look on his face. We walked without stopping. Drifting in and out of sleep from exhaustion, I kept waiting for my mother to rescue me.

The forced march went on for hours. Each footstep was acute misery. Suddenly the elephant in front of me bellowed. Actually, he **39**

H E L L O   C R U E L   W O R L D

40 *cried. But it was hard to tell the difference between anger and despair. Then the line stopped. It came with no warning. I waited nervously.*

There was danger in the air. I smelled it as clearly as I did food. Something was happening, but I couldn't see what it was.

I thought I'd been dreaming, but my eyes were open, looking at the digital clock beside the bed.

A moment earlier, I'd been sleeping soundly, or so I thought, involved in a vivid dream about my mom. I saw her standing beside the bed, gently stroking my back and neck just as she did when I curled up with her on the sofa. She was whispering to me, her voice barely audible. She was telling me that she was all right, that I was going to be okay, too. I tried asking her questions, but there was no response. She only smiled, warm and loving.

And then I wasn't sleeping. I was awake, trying to focus my eyes on what appeared to be a bright light. As my eyes cleared, the light moved away, a slip of brightness that backed against the wall and then under the door. Gone.

I looked at the clock. It was three twenty-two A.M. Had I been dreaming? Had I been awake?

It didn't matter. I knew what the light was. I knew who it was. All of a sudden, I felt at peace. Mom was okay. I was going to be all right. I shut my eyes and drifted back to sleep.

• • • • •

I arrived early the next day at the funeral home, driving by my old high school, which was on the street behind it. I remembered how often I had walked by this place when skipping out of class to hang out at a nearby Italian restaurant where we drank Cokes and smoked cigarettes. I hated high school. It was a horrible—make that a torturous—place to be fat. To be different.

I was late every day, an attempt to avoid the kids who made me feel so rotten, so worthless. Growing up in a dysfunctional family, you're taught not to face your fears, that if you avoid them they might go away. In truth, they only get a lot bigger, much as I have done.

I gave the old high school a final glance in the rearview mirror and turned my attention straight ahead. I hated the funeral home, too. Except that I wasn't arriving late but rather early. In fact, I was the first one to show up.

I read on a little information board in the foyer that there were two funerals scheduled that afternoon, my mom's and someone else's. Initially I got angry that there was another funeral on the same day as my mom's. How dare they? But then I thought that maybe I'd go to the other one, that it would be easier than going to my mom's. I could just pay my respects, get it over with, and return home to Los Angeles.

But both my conscience and my curiosity got the better of me, and I poked my head into the sterile little chapel where the service was to be held. And there she was. My mom. All alone. Lying in the fancy white box that my brother and I had picked out. From behind the back row of chairs where I stood I could make out only the top of her forehead and the front of her styled hair.

I sat down in the chair closest to me and stared at her, and after several minutes I decided I was looking at my mom's body but not my mom. A lot of people were about to pay their respects to her, but she wasn't here. At least her soul **41**

42 wasn't.

There was a powerful pull on the vine. Then a violent prod. And the line began to move.

After some time, we came upon an open area strewn with what looked like large boulders. Great pods littered the landscape. They looked real, then surreal, lifeless forms that appeared to have once lived.

Then one of the young ones broke from the line, reared and broke his vines, and zeroed in on the boulders. When he got there, he sniffed the air and pushed the ground with his trunk, then kicked at the dirt. Clouds of dust rose, visible evidence of his anger.

He let out a roar that shook the plains and thundered across the sky. Using the thousands of muscles in his powerful trunk, he tried to lift one of the boulders. He couldn't. Each attempt failed. It was pitiful. Pitifully sad.

Some of the other strong young elephants broke from the line, too, and strained toward the boulders. Though I was far back in the line, I was still connected to the others by vines, dragged, whether I liked it or not, toward the horrible, massive shapes.

My mom gave birth to sixteen. Her first child and two sets of twins died. I am one of the eleven survivors, the most appropriate word to describe us kids. Her husband, my dad, was an alcoholic, an abusive one, who expected to be taken care of, babied. We were poor, poorer than my mom liked to admit. And still her favorite expression, the one that will always stick in my mind, was "That's what I call ballin' the jack."

My mom once explained to me that as a small girl she loved to play jacks. The object was to throw a ball up in the air, then with the same hand scoop up one jack and catch the ball. If successful, you then tried to pick up two jacks, and so on up to ten. If you managed to pick up all ten jacks and catch the ball as well, that was called ballin' the jack.

She said it her whole life, and every time, after saying it, she smiled brightly like a little girl who had just won the game.

"That's what I call ballin' the jack."

HELLO CRUEL WORLD

Ballin' the Jack

8

The family was given a private moment with my mom before the rest of the mourners were let inside. Everyone was weeping, my brothers and sisters putting keepsakes and remembrances into the casket. I walked up and kissed my mom's forehead, just as I had done ten years earlier to my dad. Then I whispered, "I love you," and set a handkerchief with my name embroidered on it, like I carry onstage, over her hand, and then uttered a simple and final goodbye.

That was it for me. Someone had gotten a minister to

attend and say a few words, but I don't remember the actual

service. One of my sisters played the song "Wind Beneath My Wings" and a sister of a sister-in-law sang it. Then it was my turn to speak. I'd written something the night before, then rewritten it over and over, until it was perfect, honed down to exactly one emotionally charged page that even as I stepped forward I didn't know if I could read without breaking down.

So what if I cried. I didn't care.

· · · · ·

"It's a sad day," I began. "It's also a beautiful day, full of light and hope, which is what I think of when I think of Mom."

I went on about her generosity, how she had so little in the way of material goods but managed to give so much; about her humor and strength; about her force of life, which was so evident now in her death.

"But if I had to sum up her long, rich, and, I think, mostly happy life," I said, trying to choke back the tears, "I'd say, 'Mom, that's what I call ballin' the jack.' "

· · · · ·

We carried her casket to the Buick hearse, five of her sons and her eldest grandson. Then the six of us squeezed into a car, sitting closer to one another than any of us would've liked. All of us, I thought, could've been better brothers, better sons, better friends. But then I realized that was merely wishful thinking. We did the best we could.

On the way to the cemetery we passed familiar sights: the Third Street bridge my mom loved driving across; the post office, which we often waited in front of while my dad mailed in his contest entries; the barrel factory where my dad had worked for a measly fifty cents an hour; and many other places **45**

46 where we'd driven with my mom over the years. She liked to drive individually with her children to give them special time, quality time.

In her eyes her children could do no wrong. I sometimes wish that she would've been harder on us, though I don't think it was in her. I think she felt responsible and somewhat guilty, even sad, about us having to put up with the man she'd picked as a mate and as our father.

That was all in the past, and yet it wasn't, not really. When you grow up in a dysfunctional family, you continue to reside in the past no matter how old you get, and you continue to punish yourself for things you did or didn't do.

I knew that was true for me. And I resented the hell out of it. I wanted out. I just didn't know how to do it.

• • • • •

All of a sudden I remembered that I had thought about flying my mom in for my New Year's show. I remembered that I had questions to ask her, questions about myself. In the unexpectedness and confusion of her death, I'd forgotten all about the past that I couldn't remember. I'd wanted to ask her about my earliest years. I'd wanted to ask her when I got fat. And, if she knew, why.

And now there was no chance. Shit. I pounded my fist on the upholstery. My brothers looked at me, wondering what was going on. I turned away, but there was no escape. I was surrounded by my family, people who had even less of a clue than I did about how to lead a healthy, happy life.

I mean, all of them resented me for everything I had and I was miserable. Was I just being paranoid? Is it paranoia if everyone is really out to get you?

By the time I reached the boulders, I realized that they weren't giant stones. They were our mothers.

I tried pushing the terrible truth that surrounded me into the back of my elephant memory. I wished it was one of my daydreams. Except I knew it wasn't. I knew that my mother was dead.

My immediate impulse was to flee. To run as fast and as far in the other direction as possible. I couldn't, though. The vine around my neck and legs tethered me to the other anguished elephants. Made me a prisoner of the ugly face of death. And I was physically drained.

I probably should've looked for my mother, but I didn't want to. Something inside me wanted to avoid the pain of the loss. Maybe that would make it less real. And besides, I already knew the answer.

T he service beside the gravesite was short. As soon as it was over, I picked up a rose from the top of my mom's casket, climbed into the limo with my brothers, and rode back to the funeral home. Back in the parking lot I said some goodbyes, got in my rental car, and drove to the airport. Normally I hate flying, but this time I couldn't wait to get on the plane.

I couldn't wait to get away from the sadness. I couldn't wait to eat the in-flight meal. I couldn't wait to get home.

47

Oriental Rugs

9

My house was a white jewel on the hill. It sparkled in the Southern California sunshine. It commanded attention. It demanded respect. It screamed money, security, achievement, the pinnacle of materialism.

It had a two-hundred-and-seventy-degree view, stretching in one direction from downtown L.A. all the way around to the Pacific Ocean. Looking up from the backyard deck, I stared right at Madonna's house.

First thing I did after returning from the arctic north was to start up the heater in the pool at the hot tub. I waited patiently before getting in. A couple of days. I wanted it so hot that steam would rise from the water. When I finally dropped my robe and slipped into the giant bath, it was slightly warmer than womb temperature, but just as cozy.

• • • • •

I guess I started eating to protect myself. My alcoholic dad offered one possibility, life on the San Andreas fault. My mom offered another, nourishment. I studied the choices: uncertainty versus a rasher of bacon, a tall stack of pancakes, a footlong sandwich . . .

Tough decision.

Food became my only true friend. It relieved my stress. It made me feel better. Especially if I ate alone. Ate until I felt my stomach grow full. Or rather just grow.

Is that right, Mom?

When did I start doing this? Why did I start?

Can you hear me, Mom?

• • • • •

I emerged from the water, looking up at the stars. Or the spaceships. Honestly. I know I'm from another planet.

Anyway, I fell into a routine. Eating. Lolling in the warm water. Television. Sleeping. Or trying to. Waking sometime midafternoon. Then repeating the same schedule. One day after the next. Rather, make that night after night. Since I was careful to avoid the daytime as if it were the plague. But then something happened.

A telephone call.

This time, for some reason, the machine wasn't on. I didn't hear myself pick up and say, "Hi, this is Louie, I'm not home **49**

50 right now. So leave a message. Thanks." Then click, beep, and the whir of the winding of a tape, which, in total honesty, I had no intention of listening to.

It rang and rang and rang. I stopped counting after fifteen rings and wondered who wanted me. I also wondered why I was avoiding answering it. What was my psychic intuition trying to tell me?

I was back in my own bed, but I still had trouble sleeping. Night after night, I tossed, turned, pulled at the covers, flopped one way, then another. My eyes were closed, and my mind was stuck in some cheesy jungle flick.

Somehow the vines had come off, and I found myself wandering away from the dreadful scene of my mother's demise. I felt small, lost, alone, and directionless. I felt as if no one was there to care.

The sun was going down, and soon the African plain would get as cold as my soul. I moved across the terrain quickly, nervously, tearing at whatever obstacles confronted me—trees, rocks, thistly bush. My ears were splayed out, picking up danger signals, like radar. My trunk was raised, ten thousand muscles ready to strike whatever was trying to harm me.

If only I could find it. If only I could figure out what I was running from.

Where was my mother, the matriarch? Where was the rest of the herd?

· · · · ·

No further. My legs wouldn't carry me one more inch across the plain. And to where? Where was I going?

I found a big flat shade tree that reminded me of the succor my mother had once provided and nuzzled against the trunk.

"Hello?"

"Louie." It was my sister. "We're cleaning out Mom's stuff and wanted to know if you want anything."

"Can I think about it?"

"Boy, there's a lot of stuff. You know Mom."

"Let me call you back."

"I'm sure there's something here you want. I mean, geez, I can't believe how much stuff there is."

"I know, I know. But let me think. I'll call you back."

• • • • •

My mom said that she would always remember it as one of the most wonderful days of her life. Her father, Charles Prouty, jumped out of his Model A Ford pickup and ran up the front steps of their sturdy, four-bedroom South Dakota home—one, two, three, as if he had springs under his shoes. She was looking out one of the two big windows that framed the front door.

Her father, my mom always claimed, had set those two windows lower than usual so that his little girl, the youngest of his four children, could look out at the world and watch as her Papa arrived home from work. His ancestors had come over on the *Mayflower*. He had turned their dreams into reality, opening one gas station after another until he had many.

He was ambitious, big-hearted, and trusting, which was **51**

HELLO CRUEL WORLD

52 why, I suppose, he lost everything to a crooked lawyer. It nearly wrecked him, my mom said. Drained the blood out of his body, the life out of his soul.

But this day was a good one. He was all smiles and energy and emotion as he rearranged the living room furniture. The couch, the ottoman, several chairs, and finally his own over-sized chair, his throne. This was the chair where he spent his time, where he dreamed, where he blew air into his baby's ear, where he later cried when he lost everything.

No one wanted to look at that chair after he died. It held too many memories. It took two men to carry it away.

Yet he alone set it in front of the archway leading into the dining room. Then he went outside. My mom heard a knock at the screen door, a clatter as a lamp was knocked over, and then her father lugging something huge under his arm.

"Bertha!" he called to his wife. "I brought you a present, a big, beautiful present!"

The family gathered around. Her dad heaved the monster into the center of the sun-filled room, then unfurled the giant carpet, watching an intricate tapestry of blues, yellows, pinks, and reds roll out over the floor. My mom's mother wiped her floured hands on her apron and gasped, "Oh my."

"It's an Oriental," Charlie said, beaming.

• • • • •

Only a few years ago my mom retold that story. I'd re-marked on the rug's beauty. She had it beneath the four-poster bed, which didn't make any sense to me. You couldn't see the design, only the outside frame, and then you had to guess what the middle of it looked like.

I knelt down and felt the rug under my hands. The nap

was rich, thick. I traced the design with my fingers, appreciating the effort that went into making it, wanting to thank my grandfather for buying it, wishing I could repay him the money he lost to the shyster attorney.

I knew a little about how Oriental rugs were made. It was usually a family business. The entire family, many people, worked on a single rug. One person probably oversaw the pattern and the rest followed orders. But everyone had a hand in it. I couldn't tell where one person's work ended and another's started, and I don't think an expert could either.

The entire family was connected, interwoven, a tapestry unto themselves.

"Why do you keep that under your bed?"

I'd always wondered. Now I'd asked. I would've put it in my living room. Shown it off. Just as her father had done.

My mom smiled.

"I spend a lot of time here," she explained. "In bed. And I want the rug under me. Close. It's comforting. It reminds me of my father. It cushions my dreams."

HELLO CRUEL WORLD

Out of Africa

10

The dreams were rough.

I slept a few hours. Maybe a few minutes. I didn't know. The time didn't matter. That I was now motherless made each minute seem like a full season.

The shade tree had grown as weary as I was. A strong wind sailed by, carrying all the scents of my homeland, including grass, water, zebras, and the smell of danger. Big cats were on the hunt. I had to move.

I set out on a well-worn path that my great-grandfather had helped to cut. My mother had told me about him. He'd once protected her young life by battling fifty hungry lions. A man after his tusks had used a gun to end his life. My mother had cried a river of tears telling me how upset she was that he never received the elephant burial he deserved.

Wandering aimlessly, I fought my own battle against fear and loneliness and hunger and sadness. A vine still attached to my hind legs dragged behind me and caught on scrub and sticks, every so often slowing me to a frightened standstill.

The wind shifted. The scent of danger changed to one of death. As I continued on the path, it grew stronger, warning me to turn around. I couldn't, and propelled myself straight ahead, stopping only to forage on the ground for nourishment.

$$\bullet \ \bullet \ \bullet \ \bullet \ \bullet$$

Without realizing it, I stood among those ghastly, lifeless gray boulders from which I'd earlier fled. Wanting again to flee, I stood in the midst of the shapes and counted. There were eight.

There had been nine adults in our herd. Suddenly I felt a surge of hope.

Inspecting the remains, I saw aunts and cousins and friends. And then I stopped as still as a fallen stick in front of a withered, limp tail. I knew that tail. I'd played with it, hung on it, been swatted by it.

Instinctively I grabbed hold and tugged. I wanted my mother to get up and play with me. Tell me she was all right. She didn't move. I walked around and saw her big, soft stomach, which had often sheltered me from the sun and cold, from which I had gotten milk until one day she didn't allow it. I lied to myself that she was just tired and lay down beside her, hoping to give her some of my own

55

HELLO CRUEL WORLD

56 *life.*

• • • • •

I was jarred awake by a tremendous pain behind my ear. Two men pushed spears into my neck, while another wrapped vines around my head and feet. I rocked and bucked to my feet, struggling against them. I wanted to protect my mother from the evil I knew they represented.

"This one's a strong guy," one of the men commented. "Lots of spirit."

"A real show-stopper," another said, laughing.

As I kicked and scuffled, they pulled the ropes tighter. I was forced into another line. The line began to move. My mother wasted in the distance. Under the hot sun, she became another gray boulder rotting in the African plain. And then she became a memory.

• • • • •

Two days later I boarded a train, imprisoned with a few others in a small cage of a car. I wrapped my trunk around the bars, holding on for dear life, not knowing what to expect. The car bumped on the track, the unfamiliar countryside passing in front of my eyes like a dream within a dream.

The jungle had long ago vanished behind us, a dark line in the distance, a distant memory. I didn't want to forget it, that place I called home, where I came to be defined, formed, influenced, and shaped. I didn't know what to do with the memory, though.

Best not to even think about it, I reasoned. Best just to concentrate on survival.

"Who's driving this gawd-damn thing?" I asked after another bump in the track jolted my head against the ceiling again.

My companion shrugged.

"Not the usual crew drivin', I guess?"

"Nope."

"Where we headin'? You know?"

"Don't quote me. I don't want to get blamed if I'm wrong. But I hear it's the circus."

"Hmmmm," I mused, grabbing a mouthful of hay with my trunk. "The circus."

It was instinctual.

I was a kid no taller than a kitchen chair, if that, when I realized I could get the attention I craved by making people laugh. Especially my dad.

His two favorite words were "god" and "damnit," though it was the way he strung them together that made his usage so distinctive. He used a low, growling tone, his voice evidencing the two vices that fueled him, nicotine and whiskey. And he stretched the two words out the length of a freight train, starting slow, as if stoking the engine, before the rest of the cars streaked by.

You heard:

"Guuuuuuuuuuud-duhmit."

That last syllable finished with the snap of a whip.

One night at dinner, with most everyone at the table, I was asked to get something from a drawer. I got up. Hurried. Closed the drawer on my finger. My mind when blank with intense pain. Before I could catch myself, I said:

"Guuuuuuuuuud-duhmit."

I realized my mistake instantly. I braced for a sharp hand across my face. But nothing. I turned tentatively and saw **57**

58 everyone smiling, holding back laughter. Then my dad laughed, a real, hard laugh, and the rest followed.

I laughed, too. Relieved on the one hand. But even more I knew I'd discovered something special.

The trick after that was to know when to use this talent and how long to sustain it. Timing.

Boxes

1

"It's Louie," I said to my sister. I heard a commotion in the background. "Am I calling at bad time?"

"No, it's okay."

"How's it going with Mom's things?"

"Well, you know Mom. She coulda opened her own department store."

"I've been thinking. There is something of Mom's that I'd kinda like to have."

"What's that?"

"You know that Oriental rug she kept under her—"

60

"Taken," she interrupted.

"Oh."

"Want anything else?"

"No. It was just the rug I was interested in."

"Such a beautiful pattern."

"Yeah, I'm trying to figure it out."

• • • • •

I would've liked the Oriental carpet, but actually I didn't need it and truth be told I didn't have any room for it. My house, despite its spaciousness, was looking more and more like a museum, a showcase for my collection of craftsman furniture. I had Gustav Stickley chairs, sofas, tables, and cabinets, stuff by disciples of Stickley, and Stickley knockoffs.

I had more stuff in storage, and still more I'd bought and now had for sale in a space that I leased in an antique dealership. I had friends throughout the country scouring stores and classified ads, and I had a friend in Minnesota who made furniture crafting even more pieces, which I'd have to find room for in my house.

I didn't see it then. Didn't understand it. But now I do. With that sturdy, well-built, stylish antique furniture, I was trying to fashion a life for myself. I was attempting to create what was otherwise missing from my life: stability, shape, happiness, an appreciation of the past, beauty, love. I was so guuuud-duhm miserable on the inside that I was overcompensating, trying to buy what couldn't be bought.

• • • • •

In 1974 my mom and dad decided they'd lived through one too many frozen winters in Minnesota and decided to move to the warmer climate of Carson City, Nevada. I was then working as a counselor at a treatment center in St. Paul. (I probably should've been receiving the treatment I was giving.) I was happy my folks were leaving. It would give me a chance to be independent.

A friend and I agreed to take over the house my parents were renting. The real chore was cleaning the place out. My brothers all chipped in. I'll never forget the tears in my mom's eyes as she watched one of my brothers drive off in the fourteen-foot truck we'd all loaded to the gills with stuff she'd collected over the years. And that barely made a noticeable dent in the trove of junk and treasures she'd amassed.

I understood, even then.

Sometimes I believed that she lived for the trash she collected. She had regular rounds—Goodwill, garage sales, trash day. If someone was throwing something out, my mom wanted to see it first. She had no qualms about picking things up, except if it was dark outside. If it was nighttime, she'd send my dad to retrieve whatever it was she'd seen.

"Was that a shoe?" I remember her asking once.

We were in my dad's Bonneville, the three of us, doing about forty-five.

"What? That dead squirrel?" my dad said.

"No, I think it was a shoe," she replied.

My dad didn't even have to think about what he was going to do next. He casually checked the rearview mirror, then gave that steering wheel a yank and swung that cruiser around in a sweeping U-turn. My mom smoothed her hair and re-settled herself happily in her seat.

"Louie?" she said.

I didn't bother to question her. Even if it was a good shoe **61**

62 in the middle of the road, it was still just *one* shoe. What the hell was she going to do with one shoe? Still, it was no use arguing. I began preparing myself mentally to dart out of the car, into traffic, and nab that one good shoe lying in the middle of the road. There I was, dodging Winnabegoes. Or were they dodging me?

In any event, I got the shoe and proudly handed it to her. She looked it over with smug satisfaction.

"Well," she said, shrugging, "you never know."

· · · · ·

Even after my friend and I took over my parents' house the basement remained full of her clutter. Newspapers, pressure cookers (maybe a dozen of them), baby clothes, stacks of dishes that didn't match, blankets, purses, rugs, boots, suspenders, irons, and, of course, one old brown shoe.

I always meant to go through that stuff, sift through it and see if I could find out anything about me and then throw the rest away. I went downstairs countless times, but all I ever did was move things around.

I liked living there, though. It was a great feeling, being on my own. I got a dog, a half-malamute, half-wolf named Lenny. I didn't take very good care of Lenny. I didn't know how to care for anything. He ate well, though, better than any other dog owned by a poor person ever ate.

My roommate got a cat. Buster. The dog and cat were great friends. Lenny was always cleaning her, carrying her around by the scruff of her neck. I was envious. I wished someone would've looked after me better.

Does it sound like I'm complaining? Well, that's how I was feeling.

At any rate, Buster got pregnant and then, as cats are wont to do, disappeared when it came time to give birth. We searched everywhere for those kittens. We heard them. Late at night their mewing echoed through the heating vents. But we still couldn't find them.

Finally, I figured it out. The one place we didn't look— the basement. There were three of them on top of a stack of boxes, and reaching them was impossible without climbing over an obstacle course of Mom's garbage. After a while, though, Buster brought them upstairs, two fuzzy kittens.

"Weren't there three kittens?" I asked.

"Yeah," my roommate said. "That's odd. But it'll turn up."

Rather than wait, I decided to turn it up myself. Listening for the mews of this castaway kitty, I went downstairs and started moving around the boxes. I'd just decided on the name Gilligan when I found the third kitten.

He was dead.

Cause of death: unknown.

I got mad. I knocked over a stack of newspapers, a pile of clothes, threw a pressure cooker against the wall, and then kicked at the boxes. One of them fell over, its contents spilling onto the ground. Shit.

I bent down to throw the stuff out, then stopped. Paralyzed by surprise, guilt.

At my feet were photos of my family. Of myself. Pictures I didn't know existed. Memories I had forgotten.

I didn't have it in me to throw them away. Nor did I have the strength to look at them.

Instead, I picked up the tiny kitten who had neither a past

63

H E L L O   C R U E L   W O R L D

64 nor a future and carried him outside to the garbage.

· · · · ·

"Louie."

It was my business manager.

"What?"

"One of your sisters called. She said they need some more money."

"Didn't I send enough?"

I couldn't even remember what they'd needed the money for or how much I'd sent.

"I tried that. She said in a loud voice that you should go there yourself if you wanted it done."

"Christ," I growled, in a tone very much like my dad's, "my mom hasn't been gone two weeks and it's starting."

"So what do you want me to do?"

"Send the money," I said, and hung up.

My Childhood Train

$\dfrac{1}{2}$

I turned over in bed, a big onion roll getting stale. Where was my salve? My friend?

My arm reached under the bed. I felt the waxed paper, heard the rustle of the cellophane bag. Suzy Qs and potato chips. Together again. Like Laurel and Hardy, Burns and Allen, Martin and Lewis.

I opened the Suzy Q and split it in half, so that I was staring at a thick, straight line of sugary white lard. My body was overcome by anticipation, my senses palpitating: what an addict feels as he looks at a line of cocaine. I snapped open

66 the bag of chips and plucked out a large one. A deep breath. I dipped the potato chip into the lard, grabbing a healthy scoop of goop, and then swallowed, savoring the heavenly mix of flavors.

• • • • •

Sugar. Salt. Grease. Starch.
The four basic food groups?
No.
My four best friends.

• • • • •

I wanted to be thinner. I'd been preparing myself to lose weight for the past five years.

I used to go over in my head all the diets I'd been on. Then it became easier to list all the ones I hadn't tried.

Actually, losing weight was never hard. I'd tried to lose weight maybe six or eight times in my life and was always successful. No one knows how to diet more expertly than a fat person. The trick is keeping it off.

It's so damned difficult to change. Just one iota. I might not have known much about myself. I might have missed the opportunity to ask my mother about the secrets of my past. But I knew how hard it was to change.

I was always looking for change. In my parents. In my ten brothers and sisters. In the rest of my family. In the people around me. In everyone but the one person who mattered most, the one person who needed to change.

Me.

• • • • •

It's easy to blame other people. It's hard to accept the responsibility yourself.

· · · · ·

See, I have this theory. Every fifteen minutes or so this train comes around. It's your childhood train.

It comes by like clockwork. No matter where I am or what's going on or whom I'm with. No matter what, that train goes by. Especially in times of stress or crisis. Especially when there's something that's hard to deal with.

The train whistles. Stops. The conductor smiles, waves to me, calls, "Louie, get on board. You don't want to make the train late." There's always a comfy seat open in first class. Where's that train going, I wonder? But that's just a game I play. I already know the destination.

Right back to that old abusive behavior, that's where.

Still, I liked to think that maybe when the train rounded one more curve things would be different. My mom and dad would be more loving. My family would be more concerned, more sensitive. My life would be somehow changed, happier, healthier. Of course, none of that ever happened.

The landscape was always the same. My dad was still an alcoholic. I was one of eleven, and no one had time for me. We were poor. I didn't get the things I needed or wanted.

Then I'd find myself at the station. Usually the nearest 7-Eleven.

"That it?" he'd say.

"Yeah, I guess. Just these Red Vines and the Snickers. And oh, yeah, these chips. And a Big Gulp."

"Not a Super Big Gulp?"

"What's the difference?"

67

H E L L O   C R U E L   W O R L D

68   "A nickel."

"Hmmm. That's thirty-two extra ounces for five cents. Why the hell not."

My arms full, I'd go looking for the train. It was gone. Not to worry. It would be back. In the meantime, I'd eat. Shovel the food in. Stuff myself silly. My jaws moved, my eyes closed. Everything faded into the background.

I had to stop getting on the train. It wasn't healthy. The problem was, I just couldn't help myself.

What We Think about Before Bed

1/3

It was cold outside and very dark, clouds covering the moon and stars. As I got out of the pool, I put on my robe and glanced up at Madonna's house. The lights were on. I couldn't see any people in the windows. I never could.

I wondered what she was doing, if she was home, who she had over, what music she was listening to, what she was eating, if she was happy. All of my neighbors had such nice, expensive houses, I wondered if they were happy. Except for the asshole

70 who had the dogs that barked in the morning.

• • • • •

I turned on the eleven o'clock news, which is more like the nightly murder report in L.A. It's delivered like the sports. This evening: two gunned down in a drive-by shooting, thirteen killed in a bus wreck, forty held hostage at a bank, three killed in a shootout, three killed in a freeway chase, and one murdered in the parking lot outside a Valley shopping mall.

I tallied the score. It seemed as if twenty-two people had died that day in L.A., bringing the city's total dead for the month to sixty-three. That left seventeen million of us still among the living.

"Not too bad," the perky anchorwoman said, smiling. "And now the weather."

• • • • •

I switched to CNN—thank God for cable—and watched a woman being interviewed. She was crying hysterically. Her neighbor had murdered his family. She couldn't believe it.

"Isn't it horrible?" she sobbed. "I can't believe it really happened."

"Wake up, lady," I shouted at the television. "I'm surprised it doesn't happen more often."

• • • • •

Eventually I found the real news, Kurt Loder's update on MTV. Madonna had a headache. Bon Jovi got a haircut. Somebody new had taken Cher out to a concert; still no steady relationship in her life. Michael Jackson, dressed as a bag person, had been forced to identify himself while shopping at a jewelry store.

I wanted filmed reports. This stuff was better than thirty dead, forty hostage, two hundred injured . . .

And I thought I had it rough. Christ, I wondered whether or not I should go out the next day. It sounded risky.

• • • • •

After watching a couple of videos, I finally clicked off the television, shut the light, and slipped under the covers.

When my eyes closed, my brain suddenly opened for business. The thoughts were no different than when I was little. No different, I'll bet, than anyone else's when they settle down in bed to wait for another day to start.

We're all thinking the same thing before we go to sleep. Even Madonna. Even George Bush. And especially guys like Saddam Hussein. We're all thinking:

What about me? Why was that person mean to me? I'm really gonna get him. He'll see.

• • • • •

After a few minutes, I decided not to fight the urge any longer. I was hungry. Starving. I had to eat something. Anything. The worst thing you can do to yourself is to snack at night, especially late at night. I know.

But I do it anyway. Always have. It's as if I'm in a horror movie, controlled by a mysterious force emanating from the refrigerator. Night of the Living Bingers.

I can't seem to stop myself. Just as my dad couldn't stop himself from charging into my bedroom at night in a drunken stupor and yelling at me.

"Hey, lard ass! Wake up!"

71

HELLO CRUEL WORLD

Face the Music, Fat Boy

**1
4**

Daylight.

Ugh.

I was awakened by a strange noise outside. Not a car. Not the neighbor's dogs. Not the gardeners, ignoring a five-year drought by watering the steps leading up to my house. No, this was something I couldn't identify.

A hard thud against the front door. The noise demanded that I get out of bed, even though it was not yet two, and investigate. Who knew? Perhaps it was a baby dropped from the sky. Maybe it was a murderous trick, and in a few hours

72

a reporter would be interviewing one of my neighbors as the coroner wheeled my bagged body into a waiting van.

I tied my bathrobe shut and lumbered over to the front door. I wasn't frightened. I could be dangerous before I had my first cup of coffee. Before my first dozen doughnuts. Besides, curiosity is much stronger than fear. I opened the door, looked out, and saw nothing.

I scratched my head. Then I looked left, right, and finally down.

Ah-ha!

A box.

Wrapped in brown paper, an envelope attached to the top. I picked it up, brought it inside, and set it on the pool table. The envelope was taped down so well. I had to use a sharp kitchen knife to pry it loose.

The letter inside was a short one. Handwritten. By one of my sisters.

"Dear Louie," it began. "Here are some things of Mom's that we thought you might like."

I picked up the box and felt its weight. It wasn't heavy at all. I shook it. Stuff rattled. Probably a broken pressure cooker. I set the box down, and later I told the Hispanic woman who came by once a week to clean my house and eat my food and get me out of bed to put it in the closet.

• • • • •

Coming from a dysfunctional family, I grew up with boxes of junk. Emotional junk. Bad memories, disappointments, unkept promises, boxes of shame, guilt, and fear. Lots of fear. I always intended to get to them, open them, clean them up, and clear them out.

73

H E L L O   C R U E L   W O R L D

74   But just as with the boxes my mom and dad left behind when they moved to Carson City, the best I could ever do was shift them around. Kick at them. Stack them up in a different order.

And then walk away.

That's what I had done my entire life. I had to quit doing that.

Why wasn't that obvious to me? And if it was, why couldn't I do it?

· · · · ·

It took two strapping men with forearms like Schwarzenegger's to get the wooden crate up the front walk and into the house. Then they spent twenty minutes wrenching nails out of the sides, until finally they had the top and front off. I wanted to do the honors, though.

I'd been waiting for this for months. A friend in Canada had found me a wonderful craftsman rocker and painstakingly restored it. It was beautiful, a man's chair, a chair in which I could sit and dream the kind of dreams my mom's dad had dreamed in his.

How many times had I called and asked when it would be done?

"Why are you so anxious?" he asked every time. "It's a nice chair. But, Lou, you don't have any room for the thing."

"I want it, though," I whined.

"It's not going to make you any happier."

"I don't care. I want it."

And now it was here. I held myself back from plunging into the box, letting the anticipation build to the point where I couldn't stand it any longer. Then I inched up to it, an apparition in a bathrobe, a man with time to waste.

"If you want us to take this wood away," one of the delivery guys said impatiently. "I mean, we got other stops."

Okay, okay. I stepped up to the crate and peeked inside. I saw the chair, the beautiful, dark-wood chair. But I saw something else, too. On top of the seat, my friend had taped a Scrabble board. And on the board he'd glued down letters spelling out the names of everyone in my family, including my mom and dad.

Then, inside that arrangement, he'd glued down more letters in a personal message to me. It said:

"Face the music, fat boy."

It had been a long time since Africa.

I was led out of the dark trailer and down a ramp. Hay was scattered all over the floor. I put some in my mouth.

That was the one good thing that had happened since the train out of the jungle, the rocking boat ride, another train, and endless walks and parades. There was plenty to eat. Plenty of good hay to munch.

I didn't have any fun, though. The vines that had been used in Africa to capture me had been replaced by a heavy chain that was more painful and irritating. It jangled when I walked, and cut into my ankle.

"Move! Move!" the French assistant commanded as he goaded us toward the big tent. "Vite! Vite!"

Ahead of me I spotted a big mother elephant and hurried up alongside the imposing lady. I wanted her to notice me. I saw that

75

76 *she had a large red rug slung over her back with a chair strapped on top of that. She didn't take any heed of me. I nudged her side with the side of my head. Twice. Three times. She finally turned. Her eyes were as dead as my mother's had been, though at least she was standing.*

"Where're we going?" I asked.

She curled her trunk and pointed it toward the colorful tent in front of us. Flags flew in the breeze.

"Toward the music," she said.

"What's music?" I asked.

"Listen," she replied. "You'll hear it when we get inside the tent."

I let them take the chair out of the crate and went to my bedroom, where I got out my suitcase and started piling in clothes.

I didn't have a trip planned. I had no destination in mind. But I needed to go somewhere. I needed to face the music.

Whatever that meant.

On Being an Alien

It was dawn, an hour I rarely see. The sun was straining to pull itself up over the horizon. The sky looked like it had been gift-wrapped. Ribbons of pink and orange stretched from one end to the other.

I was waiting by my suitcase at the end of the driveway for a taxi. I, at least, have the decency not to ask my friends to take me to the airport, but they invariably ask me. I hate that.

People are at their all-time sneakiest when they need a ride to the airport.

GOODBYE JUMBO

"Hey, Louie, what're you doing tomorrow?"

"Not much. What do you have in mind?"

"How about taking us to the airport? We're going to Hawaii."

"Oh, all right. What time?"

"Well, the plane leaves at six. We need to be there an hour early. And then there's traffic. Pick us up at four A.M. Okay?"

So. Still wearing my slippers, I pick them up. I am half asleep when I pull up in front of their house. They are curbside, wearing loud-print shirts and leis, dancing the hula. They are ecstatic. They are going to Hawaii.

"Hi, Louie!"

"Get in."

• • • • •

Half an hour later, they are gone and I am on the freeway. It is four-thirty. I am totally awake.

I pull into a 7-Eleven. Two cops are inside, sipping from coffee cups. They look at me funny.

"Haven't you seen anyone in pink fluffy slippers before?"

"Must've been to the airport, huh?"

• • • • •

The cab driver eventually showed up and tossed my bag into the trunk.

"Hey, careful. I could have breakables in there."

"Do you?"

"No."

"Then get in."

"Watch it. I had a rough childhood."

We talked. It turned out he had a difficult childhood, too.

Actually, he was still a child. Just nineteen. But he had arrived in this country from Cambodia. On a boat. What a coincidence, I told him. My ancestors had come the same way. On the *Mayflower*.

"That's where the trouble started."

He didn't care.

"Why are you going to Hawaii?" he asked.

"I don't know."

"Gonna get leied?"

I grimaced. Everyone's a comedian.

· · · · ·

I hate airports. It was in an airport maybe ten years ago that I received a cold, unedited, honest picture of how I appeared. I was waiting for a plane to Las Vegas, and there was a woman sitting across from me at the gate. She was short, about five feet, and she was heavy, somewhere in the range of one-eighty or above, and she was eating Jujubees.

My favorite candy.

I watched her eat them one after the other. I watched how she pried them from her teeth. I watched how she got the stubborn one that always sticks at the bottom of the box. She ate them as if they were medicine, little happy pills.

I watched her eat them and I wanted one so badly it hurt. Then she caught me looking at her. I should probably have turned away, but I didn't. She looked ashamed of herself. Which made me feel bad.

I smiled.

"That used to be my favorite candy," I said, pretending that I no longer ate them by the truckload.

She looked relieved.

79

HELLO CRUEL WORLD

80   "Mine, too."

We felt better about the moment, though both of us, I knew, felt terribly guilty. Why guilty?

Because we knew the truth.

· · · · ·

At some point during the exhausting, obstacle-filled thirty-mile trek between the terminal entrance and the gate, I found myself standing face-to-face with a black man who was playing silky jazz on an old clarinet. He was slender, wore old clothes, and nodded at passersby. Stopping to listen, I noticed his eyes were murky and dull, just kind of resigned and dead.

My dad played the trumpet. In some way, this slender black man playing in the airport terminal reminded me of my dad.

I dropped a dollar bill into his open case. It floated down and landed on top of a pile of coins. Beneath the coins was a handwritten card that said, "God Bless." He gave me a small nod of thanks and stopped playing.

"Hey, I seen you on television," he said.

I smiled.

"Traveling, are you?"

I didn't have time for conversation, but I wanted to be nice to this man who played the same kind of music as my dad. Then something dawned on me, and I didn't want to hurry away. Was this improvised jazz the same music that I needed to face? I didn't know. I had no way of knowing. But I couldn't—and suddenly didn't want to—discount the odd chance that there was something to gain, something symbolic, in this encounter.

"Yeah," I said.

"Work or vacation?"

"I don't know," I said. "To lose some weight, maybe."

"You can lose your weight, all right, okay. But don't you forget to feed your soul. God bless."

Then he went back to playing and I walked up to the gate and checked in.

Don't forget to feed your soul. Hmmmm.

$$\bullet\ \bullet\ \bullet\ \bullet\ \bullet$$

I don't know why everybody talks about losing weight. What an ill-conceived phrase. Fat people never lose weight. That's the problem. They always know right where it is.

And dropping a few pounds? There's a joke in the works. I dropped a few pounds last week. Yeah? Yeah, they landed around my knees.

"What was that, sir?" the flight attendant asked.

I had been talking to myself. A sign of craziness? Extreme hunger?

"Oh, nothing," I mumbled.

We were on the runway. The plane's engines were whirring in preparation for takeoff. I asked the flight attendant if anything was open in first class.

"No," she said, smiling. "But would you like an aisle? There's an aisle seat a couple of rows back."

"A whole row would be preferable."

She did not smile. Obviously, she was not sensitive to fat people.

$$\bullet\ \bullet\ \bullet\ \bullet\ \bullet$$

But who is?

Being fat is like being a member of a different race. Being **81**

82   an alien. Being sick. People are fatophobic. They are petrified that obesity is contagious. They are scared shitless that they will somehow catch your fatness. That if you move into their neighborhood, they will stop exercising, stop eating properly, and begin to look like you.

You think people treat us fatties differently. You invite us over to your house, never for dinner, and when you answer the door, you say, "Come on in and sit on this concrete sofa. Or try our new steel-reinforced chair."

I always head straight for the wicker.

· · · · ·

I leaned back in the plane seat and wondered if plane seats weren't God's way of punishing me. It wasn't very easy squeezing my fat ass into that tiny two-foot seat for five and a half hours. Even worse would be trying to wedge myself into—never mind maneuvering in—the compact bathroom. These bathrooms were clearly designed with the same idea as the seats: Small is beautiful.

"Do you need a seatbelt extension?" the flight attendant asked me.

Nothing was more mortifying than being asked that question. I wanted to belt that smile right off her face. I didn't. Instead I took my embarrassment out on the man sitting beside me, who, I noticed, appeared to be taking a special interest in whether or not I was going to take the extension. I had to take it. That's the rules. And as I buckled up, I gave my neighbor a don't-mess-with-me look.

"Don't even start," I snarled, laying down the law. "I once

killed a guy just because he tried to take my peanuts."

· · · · ·

A few hours into the flight I flashed on my first memory of being fat.

I was in kindergarten, and the teacher was showing the class a new toy someone had donated. It was a white milk truck that could be ridden around the room. All of us kids stood in line, waiting our turn to drive it around the room. We didn't have any toys like that at my house. It looked like fun. I was so excited to take it for a spin I could hardly wait.

Then my turn came. But as I swung my leg over the seat, a little girl screamed, "Hey, you can't go on the truck! You're too fat! You'll break it!"

Several of the other kids laughed. Already my weight was generating laughs. I could have charged at the door. My kindergarten class could have been the only one in school with a two-snack minimum.

However, I didn't know what to do when people laughed at me then. I looked around for help. But none was offered. The teacher was occupied with something else and she didn't hear. So I did the only thing I could. I got off the truck, relinquished my turn, and, with my head bowed and tears in check, slunk humiliated back into the corner.

I was wounded, scarred for life, though I didn't know it yet.

But I had also realized for the first time that I was different from everybody else.

I was fat.

The feeling never went away, and neither did the weight.

83

HELLO CRUEL WORLD

Uncharted Territory

16

For my money, Hawaii is unlike any other place on this earth. The warm, tropical air is heavy and moist, like a big juicy smoothie from God. The air embraces you immediately. It bathes you in a tropical balm. It seduces your five—or perhaps six—senses into believing they have an indisputable right to be grossly self-indulged.

Which is why people go to Hawaii.

I love the flowers. There are wonderful orchids and various tropical blossoms everywhere. They perfume the air. Eau de Paradise.

It was as unlike my Minnesota home as I could possibly get. I immediately felt comfortable.

But did I feel at home? Or was I just running away from my troubles?

· · · · ·

As I picked up my luggage and walked outside to get a cab, I was struck by reality: There was no reason for my being in Hawaii. I was not performing. I was not vacationing. I was not visiting anyone. I was not doing anything.

Oh, I was going to go on a diet, or at least start one. And I was going to face the music, if I heard any.

Right. Whatever you say, Lou.

If the truth be told, I had slipped into a void bounded only by my sanity and my American Express card limit.

Both were uncharted territory. Both demanded exploration.

· · · · ·

I don't ordinarily think of myself as an adventurer. If I'm watching television with someone and hear a strange noise outside, sure, like most guys, I'll go after it, screaming and yelling like a pit bull. "Who the hell's out there? Come on out, I hear ya." But if I'm alone, like any other normal coward, I'll hide and wait for it to go away.

When I landed in Hawaii I was very much alone. Which is why I was scared out of my big fat gourd.

· · · · ·

I'd made hotel reservations from the airplane phone, needing something to do between the peanuts, the meal, and **85**

HELLO CRUEL WORLD

86 the movie.

"Kanapali Village," I told the driver.

Fatter than me, he looked as if he'd been vacuum-packed into the front seat of his taxi. He bit into a piece of dried pineapple, savoring the taste of sugar, and looked at me in the rearview mirror. I detected a spark of recognition in his fat blue eyes.

"Haven't I seen you before?" he asked.

"Maybe," I said, wondering if it was on "The Tonight Show," Arsenio, HBO, or one of the movies I did. "Probably."

"Didn't you used to work at that 7-Eleven in Honolulu? The one right near the nudie places?"

Some entertainers might've been insulted. I bet most would have been. I laughed.

Like it or not, I saw in this enormous cab driver a fellow overeater, a kindred spirit who was slowly, surely, and deliciously trying to do himself in.

We were brothers.

"What brings you to Hawaii?" he asked.

I noticed him reach into his glove compartment and pull out a bag of candy corn. I also saw licorice whips tucked away in there. And some chips, I thought.

"I'm dieting," I said. "I'm trying to lose weight."

Now it was his turn to laugh.

"I tell myself that every day," he said. "But it's like, I don't know where to start. Maybe I can live without the chips, but there's no way in hell I can get through a day without my Oreos. You know what I mean?"

I nodded. Because I knew what he meant.

• • • • •

There was something about Hawaii, I realized, that made even traffic almost tolerable. As the taxi leisurely chugged toward my destination, I had the back windows down so that the warm air washed over me, massaging the tension out of my body.

The friendly driver offered me something to eat. I wanted to say yes but declined. The stuff he was eating—favorites that were virtually irresistible—wasn't the sort of food I ate in front of other people.

But I enjoyed watching him shovel the sweets in.

I watched him growing bigger by the bite. His actually was a hand-to-mouth existence. I imagined him finishing his shift one day and not being able to get himself out of the cab and then an emergency crew cutting him free with the Jaws of Life.

"How long have you been fat?" I asked.

"Me?"

I made a face that was like a backboard. He snagged it on the rebound.

"Silly question. I'm just not used to hearing someone come right out and say that word."

"You mean *fat?*"

"Yeah."

"Well?"

"I know," he said. "But how many of us ever actually use that word? How many of us really face the fat." Then he realized what he'd said. "Uh, I mean, how many of us really face the fact?"

• • • • •

A bell went off in my head. **87**

H E L L O   C R U E L   W O R L D

88 Bingo!
Wasn't that one of the reasons why I was here in Hawaii?

• • • • •

"Hey, would you mind lifting your own bags out?" he asked when we pulled up in front of the hotel. "I can't get out of this thing without a lot of hassle."

"No problem," I said. "I understand."

Normally I would have been upset over that. After all, part of his job was to carry my bags. I don't ask my audience to deliver half the jokes. But I knew what it was like to sit down and not be able to get up easily.

In first grade I didn't know what a desk was. I wore one for a year.

"You're a peach." He smiled.

"And you're a pig."

"Takes one to know one."

Pizza

$\frac{1}{7}$

After he drove off, I stood outside the hotel and realized that fat people all have one thing in common: We are very sensitive. Extremely sensitive. Like baby elephants who don't ever want to be separated from their mothers.

Our fat is the manifestation of inner pain. Our fat is the result of not dealing with that hurt. It's the punishment we come to believe we're due, the protection that we feel we need. It's our lifesaver, an all-weather, 24-hour-a-day inner tube that insulates us from the cruel world and all the glares, frowns,

90 insults, prejudice, and disappointed looks that find us as if we were emotional pincushions.

But what are we hiding from?

The past? What about the past?

What we need is someone to talk to, a kind shoulder to cry on, a fat person's hot line.

Mom? Mom, where are you when I need you?

• • • • •

As I walked around my hotel room, wondering what to do next, I had an idea:

What if there was an all-night diner that served friendship instead of french fries, camaraderie instead of cheeseburgers, sympathy instead of hot fudge sundaes, a helping hand instead of double helpings of mashed potatoes?

What if, what if, what if . . .

Instead, there was room service. I heard that familiar toot, the friendly whistle blowing. Then I hopped on that old, comfortable train. Within minutes of throwing my suitcase on the bed, I ordered a pizza.

• • • • •

Forget about a cure for cancer. How about a cure for life's ills? I've got it.

Pizza.

No kidding.

Did you ever notice how pizza can make you completely happy? You can be having the worst time in your entire life, dangling over the abyss of total disaster, one straw away from utter collapse, loveless, even downright suicidal, and someone pops the question: "You want a slice of pizza?" Before you can even think, a reptilian part of your brain is activated and you say, "Yeah."

And all of a sudden things don't seem that bad . . . for the moment, anyway.

· · · · ·

But I'll tell you something: I didn't eat the pizza. Nope. I smelled it. Ran my finger over the pepperoni. Fingered the crust. But I didn't take a bite. I wheeled the beautifully arranged cart straight out the door and hoped and prayed that it would be wheeled away before I came to my senses.

After all, I was in Hawaii, listening for music, looking for answers, trying to lose weight.

I'd only been there several hours. It was too soon yet for me to lose my way.

· · · · ·

I went to sleep feeling strong, thinking about how people let their fat keep them fat. By not eating that pizza, I realized I was one day closer to being thin and healthy. That was a good way to think. One day at a time. Do without a couple of thousand unneeded calories a day.

I gave myself two years to reach a weight I could live with.

Seven hundred and thirty days. That worked out to roughly one-quarter pound a day.

As I drifted off into dreamland, that seemed like a realistic possibility, like a goal I could reach.

91

HELLO CRUEL WORLD

What's Your Handicap?

1
8

Knock-knock.

I pulled the covers up and continued butting heads with the elephant who was fighting with me over territory.

Then it came again. Only louder.

KNOCK-KNOCK!

I opened one eye, rolled over, and hoped it would go away. It didn't.

KNOCK-KNOCK-KNOCK-KNOCK!

Naturally I figured it was the phone ringing and reached for the receiver. My arm was still asleep. So I kind of threw

92

my arm in the general direction of the nightstand, hoping to hit the phone. It took three tries before my arm, like a long, fat, rubbery fish, made contact with the right object and slapped the damn thing off the hook. Still.

KNOCK-KNOCK!

Now my eyes were open. My brain was warming up. Of course, I thought. It was the door. I looked out the peephole.

It was the maid. A little Hawaiian woman about four and a half feet tall. In uniform.

"Who is it?" I asked.

"Housekeeping."

I could've told her to come back, and probably should've, but my mind was still asleep. I opened the door a crack.

"What?"

"Just checking."

"Checking what?"

I sounded uncharitable, but was just cranky.

"Would you like your room cleaned?"

"Yes," I snorted. "Get the hell in here."

• • • • •

With the little housekeeper vacuuming, I had to get out of the room. It was seven-thirty when I walked outside. Warm, sunny, fragrant. I hated it. I'd had no clue that seven-thirty A.M. even existed.

But what shocked me even more was how many other people were up. And apparently happy. I made a mental note. Very interesting. Then I went for a walk around the hotel grounds to see what everyone was doing. That really surprised me. People were jogging, speed-walking, swimming laps, pedaling stationary bikes, and climbing Stairmasters.

93

H E L L O   C R U E L   W O R L D

94   I noticed that not only did they share an upbeat disposition but they had another thing in common.

They were thin.

Every one of them.

My first thought was of a conspiracy. As I slept, people were getting thin. It wasn't fair.

I knew I should exercise, but I couldn't. Gym class back in junior high had turned me against every form of physical activity. I couldn't get over how I was made fun of from the time I walked into the locker room until the end of class when we had to take showers. I was always the last picked for a team, the last to come around the track, the last one in and out of the shower.

All of these painful memories I'd stuffed down with one bite after another. Suddenly they were coming back.

Yipes.

What was happening to me?

• • • • •

On my way back to the coffee shop, I passed the golf course and then the pro shop. I didn't know anything about golf. Noticing a bench beside the first tee and not having anything to do, however, I sat down and watched several foursomes tee off. I was mesmerized. The golfers weren't like the people I saw running, lifting weights, and working out. These people, duffers, were more like me, ranging from pudgy to chubby, slow-moving, less inclined to worship a washboard stomach than a colorful hat.

After about half an hour, I realized that golf might be the sport for me. At least I should try.

I rented clubs and shoes, bought a cap with a knitted ball

on top, and became the fourth member of the next group up.

"What's your handicap?" One of the guys in my foursome asked me.

I gave him a quizzical look. My handicap? I didn't know how to answer. There was my alcoholic father. There was my mother who fed me whenever I had a problem. There was my childhood. There was my whole way of relating to the world like an alien. I was in a real quandary.

What was my handicap? I had so many to choose from.

What is anybody's handicap? Just being human. But few if any of us have the guts to admit that.

Finally, I turned this innocent question, which had thrown me for a loop, into a joke by answering, "My waist."

He laughed.

"I know what you mean. I've got a wife who . . . Oh, never mind. You'll do fine."

• • • • •

I'd thought golf was among the least physically demanding of sports, right up there with bowling and shuffleboard and cow tipping. But after walking eighteen holes, chasing balls that could generously be described as having landed on the course, and carrying my own clubs the whole time, I was exhausted. I hit the clubhouse with sweat pouring down my face and back.

"It's Miller time," one of my partners said, smiling.

"No, thanks," I begged off. "I think it's bedtime for me."

While I was returning the clubs I'd rented, the golf pro sauntered up to the counter. He passed me a towel.

"So what'd you shoot?" he asked.

"About eighty-something on the front nine," I replied. **95**

HELLO CRUEL WORLD

96 "And I didn't keep score on the back nine."

"Not too bad for a first time," he said without mentioning that par for the entire course was seventy-two.

"No, it was great," I enthused. "I went five hours without eating a thing."

Anatomy of a Binge

19

It continued like that for about a week. The little woman from housekeeping and I developed an unspoken routine. She'd knock on the door at an ungodly hour of the morning, wake me up, point to her vacuum, and then I'd go out and play golf.

By the end of the week, I was shooting a little better, in the mid one hundreds. I was also skipping a big breakfast, eating instead a piece of fruit and a muffin, and then forgetting about my usual large fatty and greasy lunch, grabbing in its place a healthy green salad of some sort. I felt a difference in my body when I pinched my gut.

My eating began not to seem as important as before. I began to think about being thin.

I felt good about myself. Six days in a row.

And then I blew it. Call it the Anatomy of a Binge.

• • • • •

I don't know why it happened. I can't figure it out. Maybe the docs with their lab coats and their rats can help find the answer. For six days I didn't waver from my diet. I ate healthy foods. Didn't even crave the sugar-coated garbage that ordinarily makes up my basic intake. And then on the seventh day, for no apparent reason, I woke up and wanted to eat everything in sight.

Do you know what I mean?

If so, explain it to me, please.

See, I fought the urge through breakfast and right up until lunch, which was when I began walking in circles around the hotel's poolside grill, like a vulture hovering over its prey. I wasn't hungry, per se. Not for food, anyway. Love, maybe. Companionship. Mothering. Babying. But like I said, I woke up wanting to eat everything in sight. I knew it was just a matter of time till I did.

That's when I smelled hamburgers being grilled, the mouth-watering sizzle of meat and grease. A couple of whiffs, and something went off in my brain. A little click, a switch that I couldn't flick off. The lights were on. There was no turning back. I knew that I was losing control, that I was but minutes away from a double-decker pig-out.

The only thing I can compare it to is the overwhelming urge that must descend upon, and eventually overcome, a murderer. My rational, conscious mind simply blanked out. The only thing I could think about was eating a hamburger.

I *had* to have one. And then maybe another.

I rationalized the impending splurge to myself. I'd been good for six days, hadn't I? I deserved a reward. A little treat for Louie. What was one double-decker hamburger with everything on it going to hurt? Or two? And some fries? There's not a fat person alive who hasn't sold himself the same bogus bill of goods.

From somewhere in the deep, dark, sane region of my brain, I heard a voice that sounded vaguely familiar, a voice that sounded like my conscious mind. It warned, "It's going to hurt a lot, Louie. Forget the burger. Eat a salad."

I blotted it out and instead heard only the man's voice from behind the grill asking, "What would you like?"

"A hamburger," I replied. "With the works."

Ever since leaving Africa I was always hungry. Constantly on the lookout for something to eat. Famished.

There was no one stopping me from eating. My tenders kept the food coming, like the river in flood season. The more I consumed, the bigger I grew. Eventually, someone in the circus gave me the name Jumbo.

It stuck.

"Hungry this evening?" One of my caretakers asked me after the show. "When aren't you?"

I poked my trunk through the bars of my cage. He gave it a rub.

"Well, here you go, boy," he said, tossing a pile of hay at my feet. **99**

H E L L O   C R U E L   W O R L D

GOODBYE JUMBO

100 *"Some nice Kansas City hay. With the works."*

• • • • •

The works!

Mustard. Ketchup. Onions. Pickles. Lettuce. Mayonnaise. Relish. Cheddar cheese.

Oozing from the bun. Dripping down the side of the burger. Coating my fingers like a greasy glove of tasty goo.

What a wonderful, almost sexual, ring that phrase has to it. "I'll have the works."

• • • • •

Unfortunately, that burger was only the start of a binge that lasted the rest of the day and night. I won't even go into the gross particulars. Suffice it to say that by the time I drifted into dreamland, I was full.

Know what I mean?

The Leper Colony

2 0

I awoke the next day feeling miserable, wondering why I had bothered flying to Hawaii and wasting seven days in tropical paradise when I could have stayed at home and felt equally bummed out. I wouldn't even let the cleaning lady in.

I was trying to figure out, for the umpteen millionth time, why I had traveled here. What was the reason? I didn't plan on leaving the room until I figured it out. Then the phone rang and I heard the concierge downstairs tell me that my ride was waiting. What ride? Then I remembered.

GOODBYE JUMBO

102   Today was the day I'd scheduled to visit the leper colony on the island of Molokai. The excursion had been suggested by a friend, and though I'd forgotten about it, I couldn't wait to get dressed and go. Two hours later, I was standing atop an imposing, craggy cliff, looking down into the little village that was the colony.

There were three ways to get down: You could walk or take a donkey down the steep trail or you could fly on a small sea plane. I decided to give the donkeys a break and take the plane.

· · · · ·

The village appeared deserted, except for the small man who met the plane at the old cement block terminal. The man stood stoically by himself, watching our small tour group descend the stairs to the runway. He didn't move, he didn't wave, he didn't smile. As soon as I walked across the tarmac,— looking from side to side, inhaling the fragrant air, scanning the land, and sensing the almost otherworldly vibrations—I had the feeling that none of us should have been there.

The place was sacred.

I felt that I should tell everyone to leave before we began disturbing things that were none of our business. Instead I followed the group of fifteen tourists onto an old school bus. As I settled into a seat, I realized that we were in school. Today's lesson was life at its cruelest, and how important it is to learn from past mistakes.

The man who had stood so impassively on the landing strip as we disembarked was the last to step on board the bus. Close up, it became evident that he was a leper. His face seemed waxlike, his features runny and shiny.

As we drove, he explained who he was and how he came to live in the village. He was a leper, a sufferer of what was now politely called Hansen's disease. He told us that children and young adults were most vulnerable to the disease. It figured, I thought. He added that leprosy was now treatable. Drugs had slowed the spread and made living with it manageable for most of this century.

The virus was still contagious. He had succumbed as a child, and, as others like him in the distant and not-too-distant past, he had been sent to this faraway outpost. He didn't have to stay, there was no longer a law dooming him to spending what remained of his life in this paradise turned prison. Yet he, like the others, had decided to make the island home, a center of humanity.

He was also one of the lucky ones, it turned out. Often, he said, the lepers and especially children were thrown into the water off the coast of the colony because those transporting them were afraid of catching the dreaded disease. Many of those tossed overboard drowned before reaching shore.

As he spoke, I scanned the small village, the landscape and the aquamarine water, losing myself in the lull of the breaking waves. In the background the guide told another story, this one about meeting the Pope, who opened his arms and hugged him so tightly that he was lifted off his feet. The Pope wanted to prove there was no reason to be afraid, no reason to condemn.

Still, there was so much sadness in his voice.

• • • • •

I had trouble listening. Something I used to tell people suddenly struck a familiar chord. Eventually, I used to say, it

103

H E L L O C R U E L W O R L D

104 will be illegal to be fat. There will be fat police patrolling the cities. They will round up fat people in big semi trucks, using ice cream and cookies as bait. Then they will take them to a fat people's prison. The walls there will be three feet high, the bars three feet apart. The prisoners will get only three meals a day.

As the guide continued to speak, I thought of the movie *The Elephant Man*. I thought of anguished faces in Francis Bacon paintings. I thought of AIDS victims. I thought of fat people.

I thought of myself.

• • • • •

Let's face it: If you grew up a fat kid, you missed out on your childhood. You were cut off from the mainstream, ridiculed by your peer group or exiled by your own choice for reasons of shame and self-protection. You were, in short, like a leper child.

• • • • •

It's a little word, but a big question. One everybody, at some time or other, asks himself.

Why?

Why me?

• • • • •

The tour of the island continued. The bus rumbled over the beautiful terrain. Our guide searched for some of the ninety inhabitants. But we saw very few, a mere handful. I was sort of glad. I didn't blame them for not showing themselves off like freaks in a sideshow. I knew what that was like.

Believe me, I made a good living from it.

After a while, our tour guide was replaced by another. A man of ordinary build, he had the same waxy features as the first guide. He too moved slowly, solemnly. And he spoke in a peaceful tone that sounded as if it had been smoothed and shaped by the winds, water, and sand.

His was the most moving story that I heard. He started by telling us what used to happen to babies born with Hansen's disease. They were immediately taken away from their mothers. The separation happened so swiftly that the mothers weren't even allowed to hold their newborns. The infants were then sent off to this island village.

I couldn't imagine anything more heartwrenching than this, until he continued, all the while showing us the sites.

He himself had arrived while still a small boy, around seven or eight. He had come without his parents, without family. Alone, in one respect. However, he had traveled on a boat carrying other children like himself. So, in another sense, he wasn't alone. He recalled how all of the children ran to the railing as the shore became visible, eager to see their new home. After all, one adventure was about to end and another was about to begin.

And then they had caught sight of the people waiting for them on the dock. They were lepers.

The children were horrified. Some knew they were looking at images of themselves in the future, some didn't. All were frightened. Most began to cry.

"But," the guide said, "every single one of us soon learned to love them."

· · · · ·

105

H E L L O   C R U E L   W O R L D

106   On the return trip to my hotel, I thought about my alcoholic dad, who scared and abused me, and my mom, who made sure my stomach was full. And I wondered not when I became fat, but why.

Was it some sort of leprosy of the soul, of my genes, of my family? What happened?

In a Pinch

21

A few days later, a warm, comforting breeze blew in through the open windows, making the curtains billow and swirl like dancing angels. I was lying on a massage table, my naked body sandwiched between two crisp, clean white sheets while the masseur applied his gentle, healing hands to my tired and abused muscles.

Since arriving in Hawaii, I had been getting a massage every couple of days. They had been relaxing but nothing special.

However, I could tell from the outset that today's massage **107**

108 was different. It had to do with a combination of factors, including the impression the leper colony had made on me, my mood, and the masseur. His touch was somehow stronger, deeper, more sensitive to the knots beneath the surface of my skin. Though I'm reluctant to admit it, whenever I get a really great massage, something very strange happens to me.

I go into a trance. Maybe I just become very, very relaxed, I don't know exactly. But to me, it feels like a trance. And I become psychic. Which was happening this time.

With my eyes shut and the masseur kneading my body with his large hands, my conscious mind lapsed out of the here and now, and slipped into a peculiar space. Unfocused pictures, light and dark, passed in front of me. It usually takes some time before I can grasp any particular image. Names are what I often pick out. Names of people in pain.

I used to try to block this out. It scared the hell out of me. Now I let it happen.

"Is your wife's name Maria?" I asked.

"No," he said, applying oil to my calf and turning the muscle into pudding. Maybe a full minute later, he broke the silence, adding, "It's my girlfriend's name."

"But you have a son, too?" I asked.

"Yes," he said.

"And he needs something from you?"

It turned out that he was trying to repair his relationship with his teenage son. The masseur had a rare collection of baseball cards that he'd accumulated as a boy, and now his son wanted them. But he wasn't sure if his son was mature enough to handle the gift. He feared that his son would sell them. I told him I thought that no matter what the son did with the cards, the most important thing would be the renewal of a bond of lost love, lost trust.

It was the link his son needed to his dad's past and the one that he as a father needed to establish with his son's future.

I said I didn't think his son wanted the cards as much as he wanted something his father held close to his heart.

· · · · ·

What we need from our parents can't always be put into words. Sometimes we just need to stand next to our mothers or fathers so we can soak up whatever it is that makes us whole and strong and secure. I was never interested in cars, but whenever my dad worked on his Bonneville I couldn't help myself from leaning on the hood, getting closer and closer to whatever it was he was doing. I was always eager to fetch a tool or refill his coffee in the winter or get him another glass of iced tea in the summer. I wanted him to tell me what was wrong with the car. Usually all I got was a gruff voice telling me to "get the hell out of the way."

Even so, whenever I see a car being worked on, I can't help poking my nose under the open hood, shaking my head, mumbling something unintelligible, and then asking, "Hey, have you checked the battery?"

It's as if I'm still looking for a conversation with my dad.

· · · · ·

Eventually I quieted down and let the masseur work in peace while I floated inside myself. But as he massaged my chest, I began to feel overwhelmed by a rush of anxiety. As soon as his hands were over my heart, I lost control. A strange, weird, frightening, unearthly sound came out of my mouth. I'd sensed it build inside but couldn't hold it in.

109

GOODBYE JUMBO

110   Aaaaahhhhweeeeeooooouuuuu! Wwwwwaaaahhhhhuuuu-uuuueeee!

It was a cross between the laugh of a madman and the cry of a child being tickled. I imagined that I was an inflatable person and someone was letting the air out of me. Only it wasn't air.

I was embarrassed and told the masseur to stop. But he refused. He wanted to continue and encouraged me not to hold back. There seemed to be no choice. Powerless, I let go of whatever inhibitions remained and wondered where I'd find myself when this was over.

Suddenly I began to kick. My legs and arms flailed uncontrollably. Then I smelled something odd, something familiar that I couldn't identify. I cast about in my mind until it came to me. It was the smell of baby powder. I was on the changing table, being diapered. I was smiling, terribly happy, excited. And then suddenly my face contorted and I screamed.

Ouuuuuuch!

I was being pinched, and it hurt. The joy I had felt turned to terror, confusion, helplessness.

Helplessness!

In an instant, I was out of the trance, huffing and puffing, trying to catch my sputtering breath. I pushed away the masseur's hands and jumped off the table. That was it. I sent him away without an explanation and walked to the window, yanked open the curtains, and stared out at the ocean.

I felt as if I could have turned and seen who the person was who was pinching me. But I didn't want to look.

I met the old man everyone in the circus called Doc a few days after I arrived. He entered the pen where we were chained and looked each one of us over, checking our ears, eyes, trunks, and other delicate parts and making comments to the boss as he went down the line.

"Too weak," he said about the first elephant he came to, a young female.

"Too old," he said of another. "But she'll be good helping with the setup."

The next three he inspected got only a slap on their rumps and the general comment, "They'll be good for the parade."

He was getting closer to me. Nervous, I shifted my weight and shuffled my feet.

Of the elephant standing beside me, he pronounced, "This one is dumb enough to train. Or should I say, 'Smart enough to understand pain?'"

Then he got to me. Sweat covered my forehead. He gave me a quick once-over, then looked directly into my eyes.

"We should shoot this one," he said.

I couldn't believe my ears. Why? What had I ever done to deserve such a punishment? Then again, what had my mother done to deserve her fate?

Doc gave the boss a shrug that seemed to say he could do whatever he wanted.

"He's too smart, too big, and he knows it," said Doc. "You would have to break his spirit to get him to perform even the simplest trick. And even then there's no guarantee that he won't trample the crowd."

They looked at each other.

"Or you can just sell him."

111

H E L L O   C R U E L   W O R L D

112 *All of a sudden I was engulfed by this cloud of uncertainty. What was going to happen to me?*

I didn't know whether to be sad or angry. To turn violent or become a model of cooperation.

Truth is, I felt all of that and then I felt nothing at all.

The next day I stayed in bed a little longer than had been my custom. The housekeeper let herself in.

"You see that?" I asked, pointing to an enormous, menacing black bug on the wall that had kept me bed-bound all morning.

She nodded.

"Kill it," I said, sounding like the Godfather giving orders to a capo.

She moved tentatively toward the insect-thing-creature, then inspected it closely. Finally, she turned to me.

"No," she said.

"Please."

"No."

"Why not?"

"Superstition," she said. "In my belief, this is nothing to be frightened of. This is not even bug."

"Then what the hell is it?" I asked.

"This is relative. Someone who die maybe not too while ago. Someone who want to see you. Help you."

"Okay," I said. "But tell whoever it is I'm checking out later this afternoon."

Hello, Geraldo?

2
2

I was back home. Not that I particularly wanted or needed to be there, but there was no place else to go. After Hawaii, I realized that I had taken self-hatred as far as it could go. It was time to quit running.

And face the music, fat boy.

• • • • •

Okay, this much I had learned. Something had happened to me, though I hadn't had the guts to see exactly what. Maybe I was molested. Maybe I was dropped. Maybe it was worse

113

than that.

Maybe I was abducted by aliens, pinched from the changing table in the middle of a diaper change and beamed up. And then maybe they injected a bunch of stuff into me. And then maybe there was a mix-up. And then maybe the experiment was botched and discarded and I was returned. And then maybe the stuff they put in me didn't set. Like goopy Jello.

Hello, Geraldo?

• • • • •

I come from a fat family. Only two out of eleven children could conceivably fit the definition of thin. Everyone else ranges from chunky to fat, from ten pounds overweight to upwards of a couple hundred pounds.

Dad didn't count. He drank and smoke and yelled. That was how he dealt with problems. His metabolism charted an independent course.

Mom lived the clean life. But her vice was food. She was always fat. The pictures I've seen of her as a child showed a plump little girl.

If you come from a fat family, chances are you're going to be fat too. It's a cycle.

It's in the genes.

• • • • •

None of my brothers' hand-me-downs fit, so Mom had to take me to a store to get blue jeans. I was excited. It was my first pair. The store was downtown. Mom drove and we talked the entire way.

"Look at the color of those homes," she said as we passed

by a middle-class neighborhood where the wood exteriors were all painted in shades of blue and red and green. "Those people sure like their colors."

We got to the store. It was owned and staffed by two older Jewish men. Both were nice, avuncular men of a type whom I would later become familiar with. But this was my first time in a store that specialized in larger-sized clothes. I didn't realize that yet. I was as naive as the little leper children on the boat. I thought it was like any other store we shopped in for discounts and seconds.

I thought nothing of it when one of the owners slipped a tape measure around my waist. In fact, I was thrilled by the attention as he asked me what I had in mind. I told him, "Jeans. Blue jeans."

He smiled.

Then he turned and yelled to his partner in the back, "Hey, can you bring out a pair of Huskies?"

I was mortified. It felt like one thousand people suddenly turned and stared as if I were a carnival sideshow attraction. The fattest kid alive. My skin burned with embarrassment. Shame washed over me like a coat of red paint. My mom didn't realize it. With eleven children to feed and clothe, she had more than enough on her mind.

As soon as we got home, I went out, bought some candy at the corner store, and took it to the park, where I could eat in solitude, easing my stress and humiliation with licorice whips and candy bars.

• • • • •

One afternoon I ventured out to the Beverly Center shopping mall. I went straight into a department store and took

116 the escalator to the third floor. The housewares department. I found the bathroom scales. After checking to make sure no one was around, that no salespeople were going to surprise me, I gingerly stepped onto a scale.

It went from zero to the top weight of two hundred-seventy in a snap, a new speed record. Fortunately the scale didn't break and still no salespeople had homed in on me. Then I got an idea. I pushed a second scale next to the first one, figuring that if I put one foot on each scale I could spread the poundage evenly and add the two totals.

As kooky as it sounds, the experiment seemed to work. Each scale registered about one eighty, one eighty-five. Together that gave me an overall weight of between three hundred sixty and three hundred eighty pounds.

• • • • •

On the way out of the store, I passed through the men's department and stopped to look at myself in a triple-angle full-length mirror, a view of the front and both sides. It was a moment of unexpected reckoning between my inside self and my outside self, my true self-image and the jolly front I put on in public. Truth: I weighed in excess of three hundred-sixty pounds, and I wanted to weigh in the low two hundred. That meant that I was carrying one hundred and sixty pounds or more of pain. I didn't have a monkey on my back, I had another whole person clinging to me.

What I asked myself was this: Who the hell was he? And how could I get rid of him?

• • • • •

I knew what I had to do, but I refused to speak the dreaded

D-word. I tried not to even think the word *diet*.

Like every other fat person who feeds the shamed, injured, or abused child inside him with each bite of food, I knew everything there was to know about dieting. And then some. I was an international authority. I held an advanced degree in the field.

A ph(oo)d.

As blasphemous as it sounds, the word *diet* didn't apply to me. Neither did the concept. Diets only make a person thin. They rarely, if ever, make anybody healthy. As for me, I realized that I didn't need to be thin as much as I needed to be healthy. Don't get me wrong. I wanted to weigh less, to be thinner. But more than that I wanted to be well. I wanted to love rather than hate myself.

And that, I understood intuitively, had to do with my head, not with my mouth.

• • • • •

I looked in the mirror again. I stared at myself for a long time and then asked, "When are you going to quit punishing yourself? Look. It's not working. And if you don't quit doing it, who will?"

• • • • •

Sometimes you get lucky. You give yourself good advice, *and* you actually listen.

I finally decided to unravel the mystery of my past, like a fortune hunter brave enough to search the deep waters for sunken galleons laden with treasure. I called my friend Marty in Minneapolis and asked him if he had time to do some digging for me.

117

118   "Sure. But is anything wrong?" he asked, concerned. "Are you in some kind of trouble?"

"Nothing I can't fix," I said. "Or so I think. But I don't think I can do it without your help."

I explained as best I could. Then I gave him some clues —the name of my old school, some friends, and the doctor who treated me at St. Paul-Ramsey Hospital. I asked if he understood what I was looking for.

"No problem," he said.

No problem. I had only one response to that—

Not.

Gym Excuse

23

Several weeks later I received the first of the information Marty was to send. It was a photocopy of my health record, compiled by the St. Paul Public School District. Written there in clear lettering was a history of my childhood, things I didn't know about myself, things I couldn't have remembered, things only my mom would've known, things I never got a chance to ask her.

For instance: I was given my smallpox and diphtheria shots two months after my first birthday by the Board of Health. Likewise my polio vaccines. I had the measles when I was two, the chicken pox a year later, and the mumps when I was ten. The only other illness listed on my chart was "obesity."

I guess that was my story, at least from kindergarten through twelfth grade. At age five, in kindergarten, I weighed fifty-four pounds; between second and third grade I broke the one hundred-pound mark; in seventh grade I weighed in at an even two hundred; and by my final year of high school I really was the big man on campus at two hundred fifty-three pounds.

Was it that bad?

• • • • •

I had to go to fat camp every summer. I hated it. Too many rules. Like only three meals a day. One kid to a cabin. Two kids in the lake. A sign that warned, "Don't feed the children."

It wasn't all bad, though. I got to go to the Fat Olympics. I won the Hula Hoop contest. I'm still wearing it. The pole vault? I drove that sucker into the ground. I did a good deed, too. I straightened out the uneven parallel bars. And the broad jump? I killed her.

• • • • •

Friends?

Marty managed to dredge up some of the old names from my childhood at the Roosevelt Housing Project.

"It was tough on him," Tom Ribelke said. "Louie always got picked on because he was fat."

"If we knew he was as funny as he is now—and that he was going to be famous—we might have paid more attention to him back then," said a guy we called Otis.

"Louie and a fat girl named Elwanda were the butt of ninety percent of the jokes," Roger Neurenberg added.

• • • • •

School?

"He was a shy, quiet, red-haired little boy," Judy Mc-Carthy, a classmate of mine in kindergarten, recalled. "And chubby."

"Louie often seemed to be without friends," said Sybil Pleasinger, one of my English teachers. "Boys with weight problems had this same trouble. People would kid him about his weight. But he was a nice kid."

My biggest problem, according to Otis, was William Kunze, an ex-Marine-sergeant-turned-gym-teacher. He was a source of constant harassment and abuse, making me "wear a little sign that said stuff like 'My mother forgot to pack my gym shorts' or 'Am I stupid? My mother forgot to pack my shoes.' "

Although Mr. Kunze later apologized for his methodology, he didn't seem to recognize what his comments revealed about himself. "There was a group of guys, *the handicaps*, who couldn't do the pull-ups and other things like the sideways rolls or forward rolls," he said. "Louie didn't do the best job, under the circumstances. He did try to do some of the things required, but he had problems. His weight didn't help."

"Sometimes he would interject things the class found funny," added Sybil Pleasinger. "So did I. But as the teacher, I wasn't supposed to laugh."

• • • • •

I remember the doctor laughing. Well, chuckling and trying not to laugh at the nervous, hypertalkative thirteen-

HELLO CRUEL WORLD

122 year-old seated across from him. I was being admitted to St. Paul-Ramsey Hospital for treatment of my weight problem.

It was my mom's idea. She worried that I suffered from a behavior disorder. I was doing poorly in school. I had few friends and even fewer interests. But in person I was cheerful, communicative, even amusing.

I'd thought they were going to kill me. Or sell me. But I found myself delivered to an encampment of some kind, a place made up of trailers and tents and cells full of other animals. The leg irons that had bit through my thick flesh and bound me on my trip through the jungle were gone, thank God. They were replaced by a tight harness that was put around my head by a burly man who whistled a playful tune that seemed out of synch with his tough looks.

I was led into an enormous tent whose interior was divided into three large rings. The man placed me in the center one, where the elephant trainer was waiting. He watched without expression as the assistant secured a chain around my ankle and then attached it to a metal ring bolted to the floor.

"He looks good," the trainer said. "Fresh. Now bring Molly out here."

Moments later, a big, beautiful female elephant entered the center ring. She was the one I'd spoken to earlier, the one who'd reminded me of my mother. The one with the dead eyes. The one who'd told me to listen for the music.

The trainer clapped his hands, and Molly quickly trotted the perimeter of the ring, head high, stopping beside the trainer. He held a stubby stick with a hook at the end. I noticed how Molly's eyes never left the stick. Mine alternated between her and the stick.

I was learning.

· · · · ·

After watching, the assistant unfastened my ankle chain and the trainer yanked my harness. He wanted me to move. I resisted. I was scared. Then the trainer took his hook and rammed it into the tender area on the back of my leg. He wanted to show me who was boss, as if I had any doubt. But I struggled forward and passed him. He jerked the harness again, harder. My head twisted backward. Now, pissed off as well as frightened, I had no intention of stopping. I wanted to get out of this painful exercise class. So I ran until I reached the safety and comfort of my pen.

"Bring him back," the trainer barked to the assistant, who chuckled a bit when he found me chomping on hay.

I kind of trusted him, and I let him take me back to the ring. As soon as we got there, the trainer dismissed him. Then he picked up the harness and began to hook my leg back to the metal ring. I bolted. But before I got more than a few yards away, he whacked me in the head with the hooked stick. I stopped and tried to turn, but the new hook was digging into my shank again and I sensed there was no use trying to escape.

"Bring Ollie out here," the trainer ordered the assistant. "He and Molly'll show this one what's what."

"**D**o you have any hobbies?" the doctor asked.

"Yes," I answered thoughtfully. "Bowling, politics, and, uh, collecting antiques."

That's when he snickered.

123

H E L L O   C R U E L   W O R L D

124   "And you have no problem with staying here at the hospital for a short while?"

"No," I replied. "Not if it gets me out of gym."

Vampires

2
4

I checked in on November 7, 1966. St. Paul-Ramsey Hospital was the Hilton for the sick, an oasis for the poor. It was the newest county hospital. The rooms were cheerful and clean. The food was good, the service friendly. And if none of that guaranteed rehabilitation, there was the chance of medication. At home, illnesses were invisible, unspoken, accepted, part of your inheritance. In fact, your only inheritance. But at St. Paul-Ramsey, there was perhaps a cure, a transplant or a transfusion.

At any rate, there was hope.

126   My roommate was a boy who had a serious stomach disorder. He couldn't keep anything down.

I, on the other hand, couldn't keep anything out.

We were lodged on the fourth floor. Pediatrics. There were as many reasons for being there as there were kids. Since I wasn't bed-bound and could wander freely, it wasn't obvious to the other kids on the floor why I was there. So I spent the first few days answering that question. "Because," I said, "I'm fat." As harsh as that sounds, it didn't bother me.

There were two reasons for that. One, it was the truth. And two, I firmly believed that during my month-long stay I was going to lose weight. When I left the hospital, I pictured myself on a new path.

A thin path.

The new me was never going to have to be embarrassed in the school nurse's office at the yearly weigh-in. He'd no longer be the last one picked for teams in gym. He'd be able to purchase any pair of pants he wanted. Never again would he hear a salesman yell, "Saul, got any Huskies back there?" He'd be able to ride a bike without his ass hurting. He might even run for class president.

The sky was the limit.

• • • • •

This bright future seemed possible only because of the super-strict diet the hospital put me on. Six hundred calories a day to start, soon halved to three hundred a day. The program combined this starvation regime with daily exercise, which I didn't like but participated in, though reluctantly, for lack of anything else to do. On paper, the program was sheer torture, a gastronomic gulag, a prison worse than anything even my imagination could conjure up.

Yet I didn't mind. Didn't even think about it. Didn't even think about thinking about it.

Want to know why?

Dexedrine.

Speed.

Six little pills a day.

The days flew by. So did the nights. I stayed awake until the wee hours, talking to the nurses and the orderlies, and when they weren't around, I sat in bed or paced the floor, talking to myself.

• • • • •

But I lost weight.

By the beginning of December, I was down 18 pounds. And I still had two more weeks to go.

• • • • •

Then one night I suffered a momentary weakness. Or should I say my childhood train stopped by and I climbed on board?

It began early in the day. Willie, a boy down the hall with a broken leg, had visitors. They were his grandparents, I reasoned. Both his parents were in jail. Willie seemed headed there, too. He had broken his leg attempting to steal a car.

But that's what made us friends. With his leg in traction, Willie couldn't get out of bed. Which was perfect for me. I needed a listener for my speed-driven monologues, and Willie was a captive audience.

I had poked my head into his room while his grandparents were there. His grandmother had offered me a piece of **127**

128 candy. Actually, it wasn't just any candy. It was my favorite. A chocolate-covered caramel. A Fanny Farmer, no less. Summoning every ounce of willpower, I had declined the tempting offer as if it meant nothing.

Then Willie blew my cover.

"He can't, Grandma," he said. "Lou's too fat. That's why he's here."

Nonetheless, I had watched with a surreptitious eye exactly where his grandmother had put the box of candy. Just beneath Willie's bed, an arm's reach from his pillow. I tucked that bit of information away and waited.

· · · · ·

It was well past midnight when I decided to make my move. I had been sitting up in bed for hours, listening to the eerie sounds of the sleeping hospital ward, going out of my head on uppers and thinking about the box of chocolates under Willie's bed. I knew that Willie would be in a deep, drooling slumber, aided by a painkiller. My biggest hurdle was going to be getting past the well-lighted nurse's station. But I decided to risk it.

I pushed back my covers, like a vampire opening the lid to his coffin, and tiptoed out of my room and down the hall with slow, deliberate purpose in each shuffling step. My pulse quickened even more than usual. I waited in a dark corner for what seemed like an eternity before the nurses finally took their break.

The moment they disappeared with their coffee mugs, I dashed down the hall, moving like the wind, taking advantage of being nearly twenty pounds lighter. I waited behind a gurney while a nurse entered the room of a little girl who suffered from a blood disease. I had once overheard one of them say, "Nothing will save her."

A moment later, I was in Willie's room. It was pitch-black inside. But vampires don't need any light to strike, and I struck with blinding speed. Reaching behind the white sheet that dangled off his bed, I pulled out my prize. The white box was as full and sumptuous-smelling as I remembered from earlier. Showing sleight of hand that any magician would envy, I plucked a paper-wrapped morsel from the box.

Then I heard a noise, which turned into voices. The nurses were returning early. How could this be?

Then I heard the voice of one of them, this one more clearly than any of the others.

"Where's Louie?"

It was close and rapidly getting closer. I slipped my prize into the pocket of my hospital robe. I loved my bathrobe. I had never had a robe that actually fit, that I could tie in a bow. But they had ordered it specially for me. I smoothed it down, checked to make sure the cloth belt was tied tight, and opened the door, prepared to be discovered the moment I stepped into the hallway.

And I was.

"What are you doing here?" the fat nurse from Idaho scolded. "This is not allowed. Louie, you're in the dog house."

She didn't like me. I think my weight problem reminded her uncomfortably of her own.

In any event, she hustled me back to my room, interrogating me as to why I was not in bed. I mumbled something about not being able to sleep, which was partly true. I knew she was going to report me to my doctor. But I didn't care. He had gotten me my bathrobe, and I knew he liked me. The **129** only thing that mattered was hidden in my pocket. As I slipped back into bed, I palmed the piece of candy and pulled the covers up.

"Now stay in bed and go to sleep," the nurse barked.

"Okay," I promised.

· · · · ·

As soon as the door closed, I opened my hand and brought the Fanny Farmer chocolate-covered caramel up to my nose. I remembered the first time I had discovered these treats. It was over Christmas. Someone had given my mom a five-pound box of chocolates. Late at night, when everybody was asleep, I had sneaked downstairs and bit into every piece of candy until I found every caramel. Then I drank some milk, went back to sleep, and had wild dreams until I woke with a stomachache.

It was all very vivid as I prepared to bite into the chocolate-covered caramel. For a second, I thought about not eating it, about dumping it in the toilet. Suddenly I didn't feel too proud of myself. But then I grunted away my shame, told myself I deserved a special treat, and before I could stop myself I stuck it in the center of my mouth and bit.

As I started to chew, the chocolate coating melted and the caramel center stuck to my teeth. I savored the chemical re-action starting to take place. As I continued to chew, the two ingredients mixed into a sweet paste that affected me as if it were medicine. My eyes fluttered in ecstasy, like a vampire tasting the ambrosia of fresh blood. I forgave the fat nurse for yelling at me. I forgave my gym coach for making me undress in front of others. I forgave the salesman for yelling to Saul in the back about Huskies.

Then it was gone. Yet I felt better, safer, not as alone in the world. I reached for a glass of water, then hesitated, unsure of whether I wanted to wash down that taste that had made me feel whole. I took several swallows. But as I set the glass back down, I remembered something from the Christmas when I discovered the box of Fanny Farmer candy.

There were four caramels in the five-pound box, two on the top and two on the bottom.

With that to look forward to, I laid my head on the pillow and went to sleep . . . until, I thought, the next night.

I was back in my pen. My body ached. I had wounds, which the trainer's assistant cleaned, alternately spraying me with a powerful hose and gently rubbing me down with a big sponge. Every time the sponge came down over one of the fresh sores I jumped and stirred. But they were nothing compared to the laceration from the last time the trainer had struck me.

It was the tenth in a flurry of blows, and I'd let out a blood-curdling, angry scream. It was an eruption of sound that shook the tent poles from bottom to top, ruffled the canvass, and blotted out the pain that shot through me.

But then I heard another scream, an equally pained and angry cry. It was the trainer. Molly, her eyes no longer dead, had wrapped the trainer in her trunk and was holding him up in the air, squeezing as if she wanted his innards to pop out of his flesh, like a piece of fruit. Then she slammed him to the ground, where he writhed in pain.

Thank God.

131

132

In the middle of December, I was released from the hospital. I'd lost a total of twenty-eight pounds. I felt incredibly proud of myself, transformed, changed, ready to re-evaluate my relationship to the world and the world to me.

I don't know what I could've been thinking of.

I arrived back home after a month away, expecting some sort of celebration. My brothers and sisters were too wrapped up in their own lives to notice. But that was okay. It was my dad's opinion that counted. After all, this was the man who barged into my room in the middle of countless nights and woke me with the drunken snarl, "Get out of bed, lard ass!" I knew he'd have something to say about the new me, and I was right.

I was watching TV when he got home. He had to pass by me to get to the kitchen. Seeing me, he stopped. "You're home," he said. Yep, I was. He looked at my shrunken middle. He gave it the big once-over. Then he disappeared into the kitchen and returned a moment later holding an open beer can. He studied the new me once more and sat down in his chair to read the paper.

But before losing himself in the headlines, he turned to the new me and said, "Now keep it off, goddamnit."

Food for Thought

2 5

I heard from my friend Marty again. His sleuthing in and around my boyhood had turned up more information.

Apparently my doctor at St. Paul-Ramsey Hospital had developed a weight-loss plan for me to follow after my discharge. I continued dropping the pounds. By mid-April 1967, only four months after leaving the hospital, I had lost a total of forty-eight pounds. I weighed a miraculous one hundred and eighty. I hadn't weighed that little for two years, since I'd been twelve years old.

134   "Unfortunately, Louie, six months later you suffered a major setback," Marty wrote. Indeed, by October I had regained everything I had lost plus twenty additional pounds. My weight had ballooned to a new record high of two hundred forty-four. Marty signed off with the phrase, "Hello, Jumbo."

The man was as short as I was tall, but he was just as round as I was. He was loud. And animated. His gestures were exaggerated. After giving me a close look, he slapped my rear end with the palm of his hand and exploded in laughter.

"Boys," he said to the men who were gathered around him, "I'm gonna buy this elephant, and do you want to know why?" He didn't wait for an answer. "Because this here elephant is going to make me a million dollars. One million U.S. dollars!"

"How's that, boss?" one of the lackeys asked.

I was curious, too.

"It's like this," he said. "Everybody's been to the circus, and everybody's seen elephants. But nobody's ever gone to the circus and seen the biggest elephant on the whole Earth, which is just what this boy is."

"How do you know?" another asked.

"Just look at him," the boss said, pointing at me. "He's bigger than big. He's jumbo."

As I listened to this conversation, I didn't know if what my new owner was saying was good or bad, but I sure did feel uncomfortable with all these guys staring at me as if I was some sort of freak of nature or something.

But the boss sauntered up to me and slapped my ass again a

couple of times with what seemed to be affection.
"Welcome to show biz, Jumbo," he laughed.

Marty didn't mention what the setback had been. I couldn't think of anything specific. Nothing I could pinpoint, anyway. Neither did I waste my time wondering what it might have been. It didn't matter.

· · · · ·

My next major attempt at dieting came three years later when I was taken to a Weight Watcher's meeting by one of my mom's friends, a nice, humorous, and hungry woman nearly as big as I was back then, which was pretty big. I went to the meetings willingly and with a certain interest. I told people that I didn't want my hospital stay to go to *waist*.

I stuck to the program and watched the weight drop off. But best of all was the encouragement and support I received from everybody. It made me look forward to meetings. It made me look forward to getting the hugs I didn't get at home.

· · · · ·

After six months I had lost more than one hundred pounds. I was the youngest person in the area ever to have shed that much. In Weight Watchers, you get a gold pin with a little diamond for every ten pounds you lose. All of the regional heads of the organization turned out for the presentation ceremony the night I received my pin with its ten sparkling diamonds signifying the weight I'd lost. Tears **135**

136   streamed down my face when I accepted it, and I got a standing ovation.

I was never prouder of myself.

• • • • •

I don't know how much time passed after that, but I remember one afternoon months later when I pulled at every
drawer in the house and rummaged through the contents like
a crazed burglar, searching for that diamond pin. I looked in
every corner and crevice in the house. By then I'd gained back
all one hundred pounds I'd lost on Weight Watchers, plus
twenty more. My self-esteem had evaporated.

I remember feeling possessed as I ransacked the house. If
only I could find that pin, I thought.

If only I could find that pin.

• • • • •

Since then, I have tried diets. All one thousand two
hundred and seven of them.

Liquid diets, solid diets, low fat, no fat, high protein, no
protein, high carb and bicarb diets. Grapefruit diets, rice diets,
nice diets and mean diets. Every one of them worked, and
then I gained the weight back. It took thirty-seven years for
me to realize why, but now I know.

Every single diet comes down to the same thing: Do you
love yourself enough to want to quit killing yourself?

• • • • •

Check the appropriate box:

YES ☐   NO

□

• • • • •

The first step in losing weight is acknowledging that you've been trying to kill yourself. Every bite of food is a step toward that goal. Somewhere inside, you don't feel worthwhile. Worth saving. Worth having a life.

Some of us manage to be successful despite that. The reason is that we desperately want to leave our pasts behind.

But then there are those moments when the pain catches up to you. Some people do drugs. I did food.

• • • • •

Most mornings I took a box of twelve doughnuts.

Come on. It was fifty cents for one or ninety-nine cents for a dozen.

But I didn't merely like doughnuts. I needed them.

Like a drug addict who wakes up at three in the morning and wants only one thing, his fix, I regularly woke up at that obscene hour, the same hour my dad used to wander into my bedroom and yell, "Hey, lard ass!" in a drunken, abusive rage, and wondered, Hmmm, is there a Winchell's or a Dunkin' Donuts nearby?

I'm not alone in this. The people who go to doughnut shops at three A.M. look like drug addicts. They've got red eyes, pasty complexions, only one side of their face works. They have only one thing on their mind as they push past the line, talking to themselves, warning everybody to look out, showing their cash to the guy behind the counter.

137

138   "What you got in the back that's fresh? Are the cinnamon rolls up yet?"

• • • • •

There's nothing better than doughnuts. Except maybe french fries.

One afternoon I went into McDonald's for lunch. Trying to be diet-conscious, I ordered a McDLT. Then the guy behind the counter, who was only doing what he was trained to do, asked, "Do you want any fries, Louie?"

I thought for a moment, biting my tongue and trying to keep hold of whatever modicum of restraint and willpower I had. He might as well have asked, "Do you want the winning numbers to the lottery, Louie?"

"Yeah," I said.

"What size?"

Had he suddenly sprouted horns and a tail?

"How about that basket?" I replied. "How about shaking that thing and dumping it in the backseat of my car?"

Call me crazy, but I know that traffic wouldn't seem half as bad if all I had to do was reach in the backseat and get some fries. I can actually see myself smiling at the drivers next to me, explaining, "See, I've got some fries."

• • • • •

It sounds like a bit. But something similar really happened once. Marty uncovered the incident.

It was shortly after I'd turned seventeen. I'd already been arrested for my part in a snowmobile theft ring, convicted, and given six months' probation. I was a model convict, volunteering at the youth center, working at Goodwill, cooperating, and showing no signs of returning to a life of crime. Except for one problem. I had a tough time going to school. I was a chronic truant.

My probation officer usually had no problem finding me. This particular time, Marty wrote, my probation officer located me at a neighbor's house. I was babysitting while this woman, a single mother, went out on a job interview.

Tipped off to where I was, my probation officer apparently let himself in and discovered me sitting in a dark room, the curtains drawn tight, watching television and eating from a large bag of Fritos. We waited for the woman to come back, then he told me that he had no choice but to take me back to school. The day was still mostly ahead of us.

My face contorted into a tortured look of pain as I thought about school. Then, suddenly, it brightened.

"Can I take the Fritos?" I asked.

"Do you need them?"

"Yeah," I said seriously. "They help me think."

My probation officer nodded okay, and I sat in the front seat of his car, munching Fritos and smiling at the other drivers we passed as he drove me to school.

139

Chickened Out

It was a silly thing. A little thing. The speedometer on my car changed.

I was returning home from a meeting at HBO, which meant that I passed at least two hundred and fifty fast-food places on the way. Normally I would've stopped at several and stocked up in case of the disaster feared by everybody who lives in Southern California, the Big One—not the earthquake but the pig-out, that unpredictable moment when every hour spent at the gym is wiped out by the temptation of burgers, fries, candy, ice cream.

But I happened to glance down and notice that my speedometer was poised at 72,996. My house was only two miles away, but I drove an extra two so I could experience the change and pulled into my garage as the speedometer rolled over to 73,000. When you have no control over anything, little things like this matter.

Now, I thought to myself, if only I could get myself to roll over like that. To change.

At least I was working at it.

• • • • •

Inside, I took the usual route past the craftsman furniture collection that was growing, despite my accountant's protests, by several pieces each week. Then I walked by the sliding glass doors from which I could see Madonna's hilltop house—nothing going on. And finally I moseyed into the kitchen, where I opened the refrigerator with the same automatic, unthinking curiosity with which I glanced up at Madonna's. But again, nothing was going on.

I checked the answering machine. The light was blinking. I had eight messages.

1. "Where are you?"
2. "Aren't you home yet?"
3. "Where are you?"
4. Sound of a friend burping.
5. "Why aren't you home?"
6. "Goddamnit, Louie, are you there and not picking up?"
7. Sound of my friend farting. "Sorry you missed lunch."

141

GOODBYE JUMBO

142

8. "Call me. I've got the name of somebody who wants to help you."

The last one was from my manager. It was tough to decide which message to return first.

• • • • •

"I got a call the other day from a hypnotist," my manager said. "He saw you on Carson."

"And he thought I was out of my mind?"

"No. He wants to help. He watched your routine and said he saw in you a sad little boy."

"Is that a review or what?"

"He thinks he can help you like yourself more."

"Okay, give me his number."

• • • • •

I didn't know what to expect from hypnotist Peter Segel's office. A swinging pendulum, a spinning flywheel on the wall, some hocus-pocus mumbo jumbo, a holograph of Rod Serling warning me that I was about to enter "The Twilight Zone"? Instead I met a kind, thoughtful professional who overflowed with confidence as he said, "I know that if I help you lose weight, you will be happier."

I agreed, then asked how.

"It's a buffer," he went on. "Your weight protects you from something that pains you. Some kind of pain."

"That's what I've figured," I said, remembering the massage I got in Hawaii. "But I can't remember what happened."

"That's exactly where I can help," he explained. "This is why I called your manager. I can take you there."

I was curious, frightened, nervous, and suddenly very hungry, but Peter Segel was nothing if not persuasive. His confidence was infectious. And I found myself believing that this excursion into the past was indeed a good idea, the natural thing to do, if I was to gain command of my body and control of my overeating. Though as he gently laid me down on a table, I asked myself, "Do I really want to go back *there?*"

. . . . .

"It's too late," I muttered in a hushed, scared voice to my younger brother Tommy. "It's too late to get out."

Both of us were hiding under the kitchen table. I was five. He was three. My dad was yelling at my mom. She was crying, pleading with him to stop. Tommy wanted to bolt out of the room, but I wouldn't let him. It was too dangerous. We were better off where my dad couldn't see us. Then my dad's bloodshot eyes glazed over and he slapped my mom.

I threw a protective arm over Tommy and turned us around so that we couldn't see what was happening. That's when I saw relief. On the counter. All different colors. Left over from when my brothers and sisters had got back from school. I imagined swallowing them as if they were medicine that would blot out the pain and make everything better.

"Tommy," I whispered. "Look. Look at that. Over there, on that plate."

"What?" he asked.

"Doughnuts."

. . . . .

The next thing I remember, the hypnotist was handing me a tissue. I was sitting up on the table. Tears were streaming **143**

H E L L O C R U E L W O R L D

144 down my face. I felt exhausted, as though I'd been pummeled for a couple of rounds in a boxing ring.

"And I'm supposed to pay you for this?" I joked.

He chuckled and said, "We can go as fast or as slow as you want."

As it turned out, the hypnotist and I went no further. I chickened out and canceled my next appointment. I'd already been abused by my family once. If the first memory I dredged up during this regression therapy was of watching my mom getting beaten up by my dad, I shuddered to think of what the next memory might be. Why give them another chance?

And maybe, I reasoned, just maybe, I'd gotten close enough.

Boogers

27

They were ganging up on me. By telephone. My sister. My brother. My manager. My friend from Canada, the one who had originally advised me to "face the music." He wanted to know how things were going.

"I'm trying," I said, recounting my adventures in Hawaii and the hypnotist's office.

"But?"

"It's hard," I whined.

"I talked to my friend Jhoni the other day and she mentioned some new doctor. Do you want to go?"

145

146   "I don't know. Will it hurt?"

• • • • •

What they didn't realize, and what I was just beginning to recognize, is just how impossibly difficult it is to change—even one iota. I'd been lying comfortably on my great big ass for thirty-seven years. What made anyone think I wanted to get up?

I did, though, of course.

But what I later realized about myself was this: Although I was looking for change—*always* looking for change—I was looking in all the wrong places. In my parents. In the rest of my family. In the way people treated me.

The one place where I was reluctant, even unwilling, to look was in the most obvious place. In myself. In me.

In poor, unhappy, abused, fat Louie.

I saw my reflection in the mirror, but I couldn't face the music.

• • • • •

Or the Muzak. It drove me crazy as I headed in to my initial meeting with Dr. Green in Beverly Hills.

A saccharin version of an Elton John song made the two-story elevator ride too long. A candy-coated Beach Boys tune filled the hallway. When I entered Dr. Green's waiting room, an over-orchestrated rendition of the Beatles' "Eleanor Rigby" made the wait unbearable.

Here was the soundtrack to much of my youth repackaged, the guts sucked out of it. Was this a message?

Or was I getting worked up about nothing, looking once

again to put blame elsewhere?

• • • • •

"Will you still be funny if you lose weight?" someone asked me one evening at a nightclub.

"I don't know," I snapped. "Try asking John Belushi."

• • • • •

As I waited for Dr. Green, I noticed that the shelves in the reception room were lined with books. I took one down and opened it. It was a case history of a former patient, including diet history, weekly food charts, and psychological profiles. But the best were the before-and-after photos. They showed remarkable contrast—a woman fat and frowning, then thin and smiling.

There must have been one hundred and fifty books like this, and each contained a similar success story with photos for verification. There was some kookiness to this stuff. I mean, leafing through some literature, I found out that Dr. Green's father had also been in the weight-loss business, and he'd gone so far as to claim that some cosmetics caused a chemical reaction in women that made them gain weight.

Uh-huh.

I scanned maybe fifteen books before Dr. Green was ready to see me. By the time I stood up to go in to his office, I knew I wasn't going to have my photograph in one of those books. Not ever. I didn't identify. For some reason, I knew it wasn't my story.

• • • • •

But I found myself sitting opposite Dr. Green, who had **147**

148 one of the worst toupees I'd ever seen. As he began detailing his weight-loss program, I thought, Hey, this guy's so good at losing weight, he lost his hair.

• • • • •

"Have you ever dealt with the supposition that your problem might have to do with low self-esteem?" he asked.

"Do you mean have I considered that?" I responded.

"Yes."

"Doc, when it comes to self-esteem, I'm about a quart below empty."

• • • • •

Beneath all his serious instructions and high-hat methodology, Dr. Green's weight-loss program was disproportionately simple. Broken down into plain English, it consisted of one thing: starvation.

He allowed you to eat three ounces of food two times a day. And that was it.

In place of eating, he provided you with motivational audiotapes that he recorded. They cost ten bucks each.

• • • • •

I stuck to the diet. I lost weight. Maybe eight pounds the first week. But by my second visit the next week, I was so listless and lacking in energy that I practically needed a walker to help me from the elevator to his office.

"Now, Louie," he said. "I know you can do better than this."

"I'll try," I sighed, too weak to argue.

• • • • •

I kept at it. The pounds peeled off of me, like the husks from an ear of corn. New parts of me, parts of my body that I'd never seen before, parts that had been forgotten for decades, parts hidden deep within layers and folds of fat, like the Lost City of Ubar, appeared every day. I suppose I should've been happy about this.

Instead, I was miserable.

• • • • •

Why?

Because like most diets, Dr. Green's program was based on deprivation. It took away the one thing that had been my constant companion and best friend for my entire life, the one thing that I most needed and loved. And it didn't give me anything in return. Unless you counted Dr. Green's ten-dollar audiotapes.

Most diets don't address the fact that you don't want to give up food. Not one bite.

They don't instruct you how to put love in your heart, not in your stomach.

They just leave you with a stomachache.

• • • • •

I sat up one night debating whether or not to eat something. Something good and goopy. With chocolate.

It's impossible to give up a lifetime of bad eating habits with a snap of your fingers. It's impossible to lose one hundred and fifty pounds overnight. You'd have to be Superman to

149

150 do that, but even he had his weaknesses.

So there I was, thinking about eating, imagining the warmth and comfort a burger and fries would bring to my tummy. Without food, my life was devoid of pleasure. Yet I didn't want to have to lie to Dr. Green.

Christ, everybody lies. We're so dishonest. For instance, nobody will admit to picking his nose. But how do those boogers get out of there? Someone else comes in. Twice a month, someone comes in and *he* picks it.

Okay, some people use tissues. As if there's a difference.

As I sat there on my bed, deprived of everything I loved, I realized just how gratifying it is to pick your nose. It's a private thing, of course. But then you get one that's really good, and you think, Well, life might be horrible, but at least I can get a booger.

· · · · ·

A month and a half later, the results of my diet resembled the way my mother used to get on the freeway—five, ten, fifteen, twenty, twenty-five; then as soon as she saw traffic, her speed slowed down to twenty, fifteen, ten, five. And pretty soon I was screaming at her.

"Now, Louie," Dr. Green reproached me, "you know you can do better."

· · · · ·

"No, I can't," I said.

The kid behind the counter had asked if I could carry it all by myself. No way. I needed help.

Breakfast had been a bran muffin and coffee, but now it was lunchtime and I was at some multi-ethnic foodstand in the Valley, eating as if I were doing it for all the world. A couple of hamburgers, some Chinese food, a salad, some wonton soup, pizza and nachos, a couple of spring rolls on a stick, chips, and, oh yes, for dessert, a banana split.

With Dr. Green behind me, my day was a full one, a very full one, indeed.

• • • • •

I was back on board my childhood train, and it was as if I'd never gotten off.

My destination: self-destruction.

That was my family blueprint. My bequest from an alcoholic father and a mother who denied the truth with food.

If you grow up abused, the secret as an adult is to find a place where you can work out that abuse. The most successful of us are in prison. They're thrilled. They've achieved their goal. They're no longer hurting anybody on the outside; they're being hurt on the inside.

My chosen place was home. In bed. With the TV on and the phone machine off. By myself. Surrounded by food.

151

HELLO CRUEL WORLD

Salad Days

28

Five days passed before I could gain control of myself. People called and chastised me for not wanting to do anything.

"Get off your lazy butt," they said.

Lazy. Oh God, that was a laugh. It shows how little people understand what it means to be fat.

"Hurray for Jumbo!" they cheered.

I liked show business. I only had to do a few tricks: raise my trunk, trumpet a few tunes, stand on my hind legs. As if there was any difficulty to those things. But people came to see me in droves. They smiled, and I felt good.

Kids always wanted to touch me, to see if I was really real. Adults—now there's a species with problems. They kept their distance, as if frightened by my size. Or a lot of times they would hit or kick me. I couldn't figure out why.

It never really hurt, though. Except on the inside.

During those five days, I must've put at least seventy or so miles on my car, traveling back and forth between my neighborhood minimart and my home; and then I probably speed-walked some ten or fifteen miles around my house, doing the open-and-snatch.

The open-and-snatch is my favorite eating method. I'd open, let's say, a bag of chocolate chip cookies and leave them on the kitchen counter. Then, every time I'd walk by, I'd snatch a couple. Even a trip to the bathroom adjoining my bedroom required a circuitous excursion through the entire house. Naturally, I'd pass by the kitchen, where I'd happen to glance at the cookies and think, Look, Louie, a bag of cookies. And it's open. What luck!

By the end of the day, the cookies were gone. And I didn't remember eating more than one or two at a time.

That's only one example, though. It's common knowledge that nobody ever sees one of us fat people eating in public. It's one of life's great mysteries. And when we're invited out

153

HELLO CRUEL WORLD

154 for dinner, we hardly eat anything. We nibble. We make apologies for not being hungry. "How does he/she get that big?" our hosts wonder later. "I never see him/her eat."

What nobody considers is that we've scarfed beforehand and that as soon as we set foot back home, we're going to eat everything we missed at dinner, and more.

So there's the fallacy. Fat people aren't lazy. It takes immense practice and energy to plan our day, to eat without anybody seeing us, to pretend we aren't hungry, to sneak and cheat without being caught.

The truth is, it takes a lot of work to get your weight up to three hundred and fifty pounds and then keep it there.

• • • • •

It also requires a large threshold for pain.

On day number six, I left the dry cleaners and saw a woman point to me and smile. She nudged her boyfriend. As I passed by, I smiled and nodded hello. Then, as I put my packages on top of my car and unlocked the door, I overheard a familiar conversation that had always disturbed me, but not ever as badly as now.

"That's Louie Anderson," she said.

"Who's that?" her boyfriend asked.

"Oh you know him," she said. "He's that comedian, that *fat* comedian."

We traveled from city to city, town to town. I had my own private boxcar, but that didn't make up for the bumpy, uncomfortable train ride that always reminded me of the nightmare of my childhood—when I was taken away from my African home with my mother lying dead among a pile of friends and relatives, and not even a chance to say goodbye.

During long stretches of travel, I grew tired and depressed and dreamed of returning to a place where the day was spent eating and bathing and playing with family. Sometimes when I felt like this I refused to do any tricks. Ornery, the nice man who cared for me used to say.

"He's being ornery today."

But it never seemed to matter. My size was all that people seemed to care about.

"Jumbo! Jumbo! Jumbo!" they'd shout. "We love you. We love you!"

• • • • •

But you don't even know me. That's what I thought. And if you did know me, would you still love me?

We were never in one place long enough for me to discover an answer to that question.

By the time I got home, I was in a depressive funk that stayed with me the rest of the day and all that night.

I wrestled with my ego and self-image. I didn't want to be fat anymore. I didn't want to be referred to as "that fat comedian" anymore. I didn't want to be known for the way I looked. For my body.

I wanted to be known for what I said. As me. I wanted to be free.

155

156   The task ahead of me was clear. I was a prisoner of my body, and I wanted out. I had to find the key that would free me from the lifelong shackles of my weight.

· · · · ·

I wasn't alone in my struggle. I'd studied the results of a survey of dieters commissioned by the Food and Drug Administration. It confirmed what I'd always suspected, that most dieters were like me. They didn't follow a specific weight-loss plan. They didn't have a clear-cut strategy. In fact, they didn't have a clue.

- A mere 13% were on a program. (The other 87% continued to eat like pigs while dreaming of lyposuction.)
- 20% planned on dieting the rest of their lives. (The other 80%, I guessed, were going to give themselves time off now and again for good behavior.)
- Some 60% were trying to cut fat. (The rest had already cut it and were still trying to chew it.)
- More than 75% said they exercised regularly. (But 100% were lying.)
- 70% weighed themselves once a week. (Which meant that six out of seven days they avoided bad news.)
- 25% skipped meals. (Of course, 75% *never* skipped meals, and that was the gist of the problem.)

· · · · ·

It was Sunday when I woke up from one of those semi-dreams. You're not sure whether you're awake or still asleep. But something weird is happening in your brain. It was in mine, anyway.

It was as if I were finally trying to come to terms with the one thing that I'd been avoiding: my mom's death. By the time my eyes opened, whatever I'd been thinking was lost somewhere in the haze of that dream state. Yet I woke up feeling quite spiritual, wondering what was going on, what it all meant, though when I sat up and tried to write it all out, I became concerned, frightened. Something was going on inside me, something that I had to explore. But it was deep and dark, and if I got too involved in it, I feared I'd become like Cat Stevens.

I tried anyway.

I put pencil to paper and closed my eyes, letting the spirit guide my hand.

When I opened my eyes, a single word was jotted neatly on the pad of paper; a word that wasn't even in my vocabulary; a word that I had previously uttered only to ask if it was included with my entree. But it was *the* word.

• • • • •

Salad

• • • • •

Salad?

Some people's stomachs growl. Mine let out a long, mournful sorrow-filled groan. I had to search long and hard even to find salad on my list of preferred foods. And when I did finally locate it, salad—even with ranch dressing—was a notch below that other favorite of mine, communion wafers.

I've always wondered why they don't put a little flavoring on those wafers. A daub of frosting? Some powdered sugar? **157**

158 I mean, could anyone think God would be opposed to some flavoring? Does anyone think He's up there eating those wafers?

I guarantee that if God wants lobster, it's fresh lobster every night. All He has to do is snap his fingers, and the lobster is right there. You're dead. You're cooked. I'm eating you. Goodbye. Pass the butter sauce.

• • • • •

However, at the grocery store, I loaded up my cart without a trace of guilt. Fresh romaine lettuce. Iceberg lettuce. Tomatoes. Broccoli. Celery. Carrots. Radishes. Several cans of white tuna. Lemons . . .

I figured that I had at least thirty-five pounds of food in the cart. Miraculously, though, it totaled only slightly more than one hundred calories—less than half a Mrs. Field's cookie or five spoonfuls of ice cream.

And with that, I entered my salad days.

If I couldn't stop eating, I'd at least stop eating junk and substitute salad in its place.

Which I did. Breakfast. Lunch. And dinner. Before I knew it, I began to crave these salads.

• • • • •

Then I did the unthinkable.

I did it after speaking to my older brother Jim, who called to tell me that a guy both of us knew back home had died.

"He was forty-three," Jim said.

I was shocked. Christ, I thought, in six years I'll be that age. People will say, "Hey, that fat comedian died."

"How're you doing otherwise?" Jim asked.

I barely heard the question. I was still lost in the fog of surprise. But with a born-again fervor, I replied, "I want to live!"

Shortly afterward, my brother hung up. And that's when it happened. I committed myself to exercise.

I ordered a treadmill.

The circus pulled up stakes and left town, leaving me behind in my pen. Actually, it was no longer a pen. Merely a spike rammed into the middle of a dusty field. I was connected to the spike by a few feet of chain.

It was lonely, but not all bad. For the first time, I felt as if I were back in Africa. An open field. The hot sun. The smell of nature filtering through the humid air. I thought about the journey that had brought me here. The trailer. The train. The boat. I hoped beyond hope that somehow I was going to return home.

Such wasn't to be my fate, though. I'd been sold to the promoter of a different circus. Supposedly the biggest circus anywhere, and they wanted me, really wanted me, because of my gigantic size.

"You call him Jumbo?" the promoter who bought me had mused during the negotiations. "I like it. I like him."

Maybe, I thought upon hearing this, I wouldn't get beaten at this new circus. I hoped not. Despite my longing to return home, I was, I had to admit, kind of getting to like the hoopla and attention that greeted me.

It was sort of like dessert. Once you taste the roar of the crowd, you don't ever want it to stop.

159

HELLO CRUEL WORLD

160

The first payoff from all the effort I was expending occurred in a place I would've considered unlikely—onstage. I was performing at the Comedy and Magic Club in
Hermosa Beach. During my routine, I did a bit about Foto-
mats. "What do they do for breaks?" I asked. "Shut the little
window and duck down where no one can see them?"

As I said this, I mimed the action, pretending to close the
window and then squatting down. Ordinarily, I bent my knees
slightly. Just enough to get the point across. But this time, I
went into a full squat. I didn't even think about it. I just
lowered myself down. And then I nearly started to cry. Because it didn't hurt. Nor was it hard to get up.

The sense of triumph I felt was overwhelming. It was if
I'd taken my first steps. Baby steps.

Now, I figured, it was only a matter of time before I got
up the courage and coordination to run.

Miles from Nowhere

29

I started out doing half a mile on the tread-mill. It was ungodly hard. Harder than anything I'd ever attempted. Including laps in high school gym class. The sweat poured out of me. My breathing tripled. My heart beat like a jackhammer trying to break through a slab of concrete, and I worried that the stitch in my side was the beginning of cardiac arrest.

Step, gasp, step, gasp, step, gasp, gasp, gasp . . .

Thoughts swirled in my head: Should I finish the half mile? Should I call 911 and report an emergency? Or should

161

162 I forget the treadmill, drive to the local Soup Exchange, and eat a platter of the crispy cheese bread?

Step, gasp, step, gasp, gasp, gasp, step . . .

After a week of diet and exercise, I realized that I didn't have to worry about getting thin.

I was going to drop dead from trying.

· · · · ·

Three times in one week I woke at eight A.M. to exercise. No kidding. The sound of my alarm was like electroshock therapy. I finally opened my eyes at around eight-twenty. Ten minutes later, my brain began to sputter and function, demanding to know what the hell was going on.

I didn't have an answer.

By nine, though, I was on the treadmill. I trudged, cursed, ached, and sweated my way past a half mile, walking a mile in about nineteen minutes. Christ, I thought, if only I could make myself exercise with the same zeal with which I ate.

Then came a challenge that was harder than exercise—change.

It wasn't even a contest. The exercise, the salad—that was one thing. But real change was another. I couldn't believe, I couldn't begin to understand, how excruciatingly difficult it was to love myself. Every bite of food I didn't take, every step I logged on the treadmill, was an effort in loving myself.

Yet it was so painful.

Step, gasp, step, gasp, gasp, gasp . . .

Every breath was an attempt to live. Every gasp brought me back to square one, to the core issue of my life, to the fundamental questions I had wanted to ask my mother before she died.

What had happened to me? What had actually occurred to make me not like myself? How had I become such a glutton for self-punishment? And what had made me so incredibly resistant to change?

• • • • •

I was chugging along on the mill, passing the half-mile mark and heading, I hoped, for a new record of two miles. The sweat rained out of every pore of my fat but thinning body. Between breaths, I chanted a self-styled mantra: "I am not my body, I am free. I am not my body, I am free. . . ."

All the while, I fought visions of Twinkies and sour-cream-'n'-onion tortilla chips.

Then the phone rang.

I jumped off the treadmill faster than you can say, "Would you like any fries with that?"

"Hello?" I said, though my brain was rejoicing, "Thank God you called, whoever you are."

It turned out to be Jim. We chatted some, the meaningless stuff that always precedes the meat and potatoes of a family call. I waited nervously, warily.

No matter how far you distance yourself from your family—especially when you come from a dysfunctional one—no matter how free you think you are from them, they can reel you back in, filet you, and stick you on a hot skillet with the speed and expertise of Wolfgang Puck. It happens so effortlessly that you don't even realize you've been fried.

"I wanted to tell you that I'm making a pretty big change in my life," he said.

Right away, I was jealous.

"Jackie and I are getting a divorce," he said.

163

H E L L O   C R U E L   W O R L D

164   I wasn't jealous anymore.

"Listen," I said. "Why don't you come out to L.A. and stay with me for a while?"

"I don't know."

"Think about it."

"All right," he said. "I'll do that."

• • • • •

I wanted to be under three hundred pounds by the fall. With the program I was keeping, it seemed like a realistic goal. Exercise and salad. More salad and more exercise. I remembered when I wanted to be under three-fifty and everybody else I knew just wanted me to get below four hundred.

"Don't worry," I'd said, surliness intended. "I'm not going to fall on you. You won't have to carry the casket."

• • • • •

It was hard for me to relate to other people. That was one thing I knew without having to be told. However, as I continued to thin down, I began to examine why that was. My weight was a demilitarized zone between me and the rest of the world, an unbridgeable barrier against intimacy. If I was fat, I reasoned, then nobody would want to love me. And that gave me even more reason to eat. Being loved by food had always been safer than being loved by people.

Christ, I must've been hurt badly to trust food more than people.

• • • • •

I cracked the mile barrier while watching Janis Joplin belt out "Piece of My Heart." I'd bought a videotape of her performing. She looked like the drunken, doped-out, over-decorated sixties diva she was. But I loved her. Her passion. And her voice. That voice. What a voice! She sang what many people feel. With rage, depression, shame, a longing to be loved, and a self-hatred that turned away everything and everybody.

Like my weight.

Watching her, I thought about how easy it would've been for me to latch on to drugs. It just so happened I found succor, medication, and love in food. But if it had been drugs, I have no doubt that I would've been gone by now. Long gone.

I was very much alive, though. The treadmill clicked off a second mile. I felt good. I wanted to keep walking.

"Go forward," I urged myself. "Don't look back."

I looked at every mile as a mile of love. Forty minutes of hugging myself, burning two hundred and fifty calories of the past. Every step brought me that much closer to a smaller waist and a bigger heart.

The more I loved me, the more I could be loved.

• • • • •

Then I suffered a setback. It was inevitable, I guess, because we rarely learn from our successes. Knowledge and wisdom usually arise from our mistakes. But still, that didn't comfort me when I took a risk and was rejected. I wanted to be with someone, and I didn't get the response I wanted. It didn't merely hurt, it crushed me.

Afterward, I stood outside a restaurant, staring at my car. The valet had parked it curbside and was motioning me to come. A single street lamp illuminated the area. I felt as if I were on a movie set. As I walked toward my car, a transfor-

165

mation took place. It turned into a train, my childhood train.

"All aboard!" the conductor yelled.

I was torn.

I wanted to take my familiar seat. I knew what to expect from the ride. Comfort. Ease.

Yet I knew what the consequences would be if I did, and that was exactly what I was trying to escape.

I slipped the conductor—er, the valet—a couple of dollars and started the ignition. I was in a quandary, still uncommitted about whether to drive or take the train. But then I heard a voice from my past, a voice that sounded hauntingly similar to my dad's, and it told me, "Get on the train, before I kick your ass."

I didn't love the circus so much as I was resigned to it. It was my fate.

Or was it? Can you change fate?

If you can't, then what's the use in going on? In dreaming dreams?

At any rate, the circus was a good enough place for those of us who were different from everyone else. Constantly on the move. Never getting to know anybody. Running from our families. From our roots. From the truth.

It was easy. Do a show. Get on the train.

Why, then, did I spend every night in my boxcar wishing I could get off?

Later that night, I arrived at a mighty familiar station, a destination where I didn't want to be—on my bed, surrounded by the comfort and warmth of items guaranteed to relieve loneliness, misery, and alienation, if only temporarily: two doughnuts, peanut brittle, two Taco Bell grandes, sugar-coated crispas, two pieces of chicken, a Kit Kat, and a Häagen-Dazs bar that would serve as a good-night kiss.

I couldn't believe I was back where I was before. Maybe not as far back as before. But I thought of all the miles I had logged on the treadmill during the last three months. For what?

I was still miles from nowhere.

The Meaning of Life

3
0

All right, all right already. It wasn't all for nothing. It wasn't like I hadn't gone anywhere.

I had a bad night. A couple of bad nights. But I ask you, "Have you ever been betrayed by a Hostess cherry pie?"

Eventually, though, I got back on the treadmill and started eating salads again.

Part of me was getting something out of this, and part of me wasn't. Physically, I could feel the difference. Even better, I could see it. If I'd been forced to estimate, I would've guessed that I'd lost somewhere between forty and sixty pounds in the previous few months. I was exercising and watching the foods I ate, though I tried now and then to treat myself with a few of my favorite candies. However, I was only teasing—and even torturing—myself. Pretty soon I was on the verge of losing control again.

It was a real battle between me and the calories, a constant fight.

I wondered if I would've been under three hundred pounds already if I'd been on one of the popular diet plans. Maybe. Probably. But then what? I probably would have told myself, "Okay, Louie, you're thinner now. You can eat whatever you want." I might've then gained it all back. Might've? Hell, I *would* have. And that would have been a hell of a blow.

See, what I realized was that diet and exercise were having a positive effect. But I still didn't have it together emotionally. My childlike psyche was still tender and bruised. That part of me wasn't responding to the new health regime at all.

The trainer led me back to the pen. I could still hear the crowd calling my name: "Jumbo! Jumbo! Jumbo!" The trainer pitched several bales of fresh golden hay into the pen and threw in a half-dozen apples, too. "Jumbo! Jumbo!" the crowd continued to chant.

The owner of the circus wandered in and slung his arm around the trainer. "Goddamn, I love this guy," he said, gesturing toward me. "I love this big animal." Then he patted me on the rump. "If I had more like you, Jumbo," he said, smiling, "I'd be on Easy Street."

I raised my trunk and trumpeted a happy thank you.

169

H E L L O   C R U E L   W O R L D

170

I still couldn't get around one basic truth of my existence: Whenever I ate—exercise and salads be damned—I felt better. It was as simple as that. I didn't make that up in my head. Or my stomach. It was fact. I was willing to wager, too, that almost every other person with a weight problem felt the same way.

Hungry.

Insatiably hungry.

Not so much for food. We could live off reserves for an extended period.

No, we craved something else. And that, I began to see, was the real key.

Love.

• • • • •

The amount of love you get during childhood is proportionate to the amount of life you can handle.

If you don't get any love, you can't handle life. Period. There's nothing to fall back on. No security, self-esteem, strength. No nothing. And so you spend every day for the rest of your life, like a rat on a Habitrail, trying to compensate for this deficiency. Which is where drugs—or food, in my case—enters the picture.

• • • • •

The key to dieting is inner strength. The key to acquiring inner strength is self-love.

I didn't love myself. I had to figure out why. And then I

had to figure out how to change it.

· · · · ·

In the meantime, another letter from Marty arrived. It had been a while since I'd heard from him. He'd moved on from investigating my early, formative years to checking out my family's history. His letter said that there were eight thousand stories in the Anderson family history. He wanted to know which ones I wanted him to dig up and send.

I replied, "All of them."

· · · · ·

I didn't work much. I repeatedly told my agent, my manager, and anyone else who called, "No, I'm way too busy."

I wasn't lying, either.

In addition to concentrating on eating salads and running up the mileage on my treadmill odometer, I watched a lot of television. I admit it, I loved to watch TV, especially—and I know this is sick—"Wheel of Fortune."

That damn wheel was just another item on my ever-growing list of addictions. But it made me feel good in the same way a bag of candy corn or red licorice did.

· · · · ·

"There's more to 'Wheel' than you might think," I explained to my business manager, whose calls were more frequent than Vanna's outfit changes as he tried to persuade me to perform more often. "It says a lot about life. In a metaphoric way, of course."

"Louie, you're not only losing money," he said. "I think you're losing your head."

171

HELLO CRUEL WORLD

"Good," I cracked. "That's ten more pounds."

He didn't get it. I continued with my lecture, having become a fairly serious student of the show. " 'Wheel,' " I observed, "overflows with hand clapping and good cheer. The contestants are all out-of-their-mind happy. Happy to the point of being both spastic and stupid. Seriously. Just think about how many people have trouble spinning that wheel. For Christ's sake, is there a guy in the back tightening the wheel up?

"Then, no matter what, whenever there's a three-letter word—and there's already a *T* and an *H* on the board,—the contestant inevitably says, 'I think I'll buy an *E*, Pat.' I mean, what else could it be? *Thr? Thm? Thq?* Just once I'd like to see Pat exclaim, 'Duh! You know, you're so damn stupid! I thought Vanna was dumb. Get the hell out of here!' "

But "Wheel" is real life. A microcosm, perhaps. But real.

And in real life people are stupid.

And in real life people lie.

That's the biggest lesson "Wheel" offers. All the players are screaming for one another. "Come on, Judy! Big money! Money, money, money! Come on, Judy! Win big!" Of course, what they're really thinking is, "Screw up, Judy! Buy that *Q*. Think *Thq*. Screw up, Judy. Cuz I'm next. I'm next. And that money's gonna be mine!"

That's real life.

$$\bullet \ \bullet \ \bullet \ \bullet \ \bullet$$

There were rumors about me. Not in the tabloids, but among my friends.

My buddy Bob came over one afternoon and plopped down on one of my craftsman couches. He asked what I'd been up to. I pointed to the treadmill and a bottle of low-cal salad dressing and then held up the remote control.

"You know, Louie," he said sadly, "you're wasting your life."

I disagreed. But rather than get into a protracted argument, I got right to the point. From watching "Wheel of Fortune," I said, I'd come up with the answer to the question that had befuddled philosophers, wise men, dictators, and game show contestants, and even him, Bob, from the beginning of time.

Bob raised his eyebrows, anticipating the punchline.

"Yes?"

"I came up with the meaning of life," I said with a finality and confidence that left no opening for a rejoinder.

"And?"

"And what the meaning of life comes down to," I said slowly, "is the whole love thing."

"Ah, Louie," he said. "You might look like Buddha, but do you—"

"No, let me explain," I interrupted. "It sounds silly, I know. It sounds so incense, puka shells, and Birkenstocks. I know that, too."

"So Grateful Dead. So . . . so goddamn seventies."

"So what," I said, annoyed. "Listen. If people had more patience with each other, if people acted with more care, concern, and compassion for each other, if people quit BSing and lying to each other and were more *honest* with each other, then it seems there wouldn't be so many, if any, problems."

Bob looked at his watch. He knew I'd lost my marbles and he had no patience for any more of my ramblings. He headed for the door.

173

H E L L O   C R U E L   W O R L D

174   "Call me crazy," I said, shrugging.
"Lou," he said before leaving. "You sound so bitter."
"I'm not bitter," I said. "I'm just hungry."

• • • • •

I was right, though. The truth is that all of us are the same and all of us want the same thing.

Love.

We want to be swaddled, cooed at, touched, and pampered as if we were newborns in a crib.

If everybody gave it, then everybody would receive it.

And that's the meaning of life.

Everything else is bologna, nothing more than a consolation prize for showing up.

• • • • •

Maybe I was turning into the Cat Stevens of comedy. I began to tell people how I felt about them. In clubs. In checkout lines. In drive-thrus.

"I love you, man."

I'd get a strange look.

"What the hell are you talking about?"

"I love you."

"Christ, get the hell away from me."

I knew it would be hard, but . . .

"Tell everyone you love them!"

"Call the cops! This guy's crazy!"

• • • • •

Oddly enough, I found myself thinking about my family. None of them had called for a while. Not a word. Which was very strange. Then again, I hadn't called either. I hadn't been home since my mom's funeral.

However, late one night I called my brother Jim and suggested again that he come stay with me in L.A. for a few weeks. I knew the change of scenery would do him good. It would do me good, too. But I didn't mention that part.

"What am I going to do for a couple weeks?" he asked.

"I don't know," I said. Then after a moment's thought, I added, "You could build a deck."

As for me, I planned on building a relationship.

HELLO CRUEL WORLD

Food for Thought

From birth, I could see into the future. That's what it's like when you're the tenth of eleven children. It wasn't an extrasensory thing. That came later. But my life was mapped out pretty clearly. From observing my older brothers and sisters, I could get some idea of how I was going to look and act five, ten, and even fifteen years later.

I knew I was going to be fat. I knew I was in for trouble.

As a result, I was more than surprised at how my brother Jim looked when he arrived at my house. He'd lost some weight. Equally important—perhaps more so—he appeared to be happy and content. At ease. Inside and out.

The irony is that before Jim even got to my house, the phone calls from the family started. A couple of sisters. A brother. They all wanted to know the same thing. Did I think Jim was okay?

"What do you mean?"

"Well, how is he?"

"I don't know," I said. "He's not even here yet."

"Let us know then, all right?"

"Why? What's the matter?"

"You know. The divorce. His job. Just everything."

"Okay," I said. "I'll let you know. Talk to you later."

I couldn't wait to hang up.

"Wait, wait," they said. "How are you? You don't sound too good yourself."

"Oh, that's just my stomach growling."

• • • • •

I couldn't deal with that stuff.

The glue that held my family—most families—together was too sticky for me.

If only I'd learned something from my dad. My dad knew how to handle the family. In any situation. His mastery was best exemplified by his driving. He always drove. Dads never want anyone else to drive. Mine especially. On his way out the door, he'd announce, "I'll do the goddamn driving. I was in a war!"

That was his blanket excuse. He picked what we watched on our one TV. He decided where we'd eat dinner. He tormented us in his drunken jags. He determined whether we'd cry or laugh. Why?

177

HELLO CRUEL WORLD

178   Goddamnit, he was in a war!

· · · · ·

"I feel like I just got out of a goddamned war," Jim said with a sigh.

"I know what you mean. But you look great."

"Think so?"

For once I wasn't lying.

Jim was fifty. His features pure Anderson. His disposition also pure Anderson. As I said, it was like looking into a crystal ball and seeing the future. I felt hopeful. Maybe there *was* a chance in hell for me.

I showed my brother around the house, pointing out only the things I thought he'd be interested in. The pool table. Madonna's house on the hill above mine. The telescope I'd bought to look up at her place.

"You ever see her?" he asked.

"Only on MTV," I said.

We finished up the tour in the living room, with me pointing out the numerous pieces of craftsman furniture I treasured so much. Jim studied each piece as I described it. He built things. He was good with his hands. I thought he'd appreciate the furniture. I guessed right. He immediately kicked back on a Stickley sofa.

"Hey," I whined. "That's worth twenty-five grand."

"Sorry, Louie. I thought it was for sitting on."

Then it was my turn to apologize. He had a point that even Gustav Stickley, the furniture maker, wouldn't have argued with. It was a couch, first and foremost, and it always would be. That was its value. It was a couch that was made well. I'd assigned some other value to it, something much greater than it actually possessed, something that, in truth, was meaningless. I just didn't quite understand that yet.

Something else caught Jim's eye. He swung around as if he'd seen a ghost.

"Jesus H. Christ, Louie!" he exclaimed, pointing. "What the hell is that over there?"

"That?" I asked.

"That," he said.

"It's my treadmill."

Jim nearly doubled over from laughter. His reaction made it appear that I'd told the best joke of my life. Given how sporadic my use of it had become, maybe I had. In any event, I explained that I tried to get on the contraption once a day and walk for two miles. Jim scratched his head in bewilderment. He tried to make sense of it all. He looked at me, at the treadmill, then back at me.

"What the hell are you trying to do to yourself?"

● ● ● ● ●

Standing out by the pool, I explained. I had thought about the deck so much that when I shut my eyes it was as if it was already built. Jim took mental notes as I described how I wanted the redwood deck to jut over the hillside.

"You've already got this great patio," he said. "Why do you need this extra deck?"

"Because I want it," I said, sounding more and more like the little brother I was.

He questioned me with the same look I use onstage.

"Okay. I want the deck because I want to do something with my life."

Jim laughed.

179

H E L L O   C R U E L   W O R L D

180

"Isn't that just like you, Louie?"

"What?" I whined.

"You want to do something with your life, so you get someone else—in this case, me—to do it for you."

"Stop picking on me."

"Listen," he said. "If I've learned anything over the past year of my life, which hasn't been pleasant, I've learned one thing. You have to take responsibility for your own actions. You have to do things for yourself."

A clutch of anxiety took hold of me. Jim had given me food for thought. Yet I found myself suddenly craving a submarine sandwich and a bag or two of chips. Here it was. I heard the train pull into the station. Time to go. I fought the urge, though, and instead climbed onto the treadmill while Jim borrowed my car and went to the lumber store.

· · · · ·

The more time I spent with Jim, the more I admired him. He was in a period of transition, and he was dealing with it. Thriving on it, in fact. Jim had done lots of things in his life. He'd painted houses. Done construction. Counseled children. Worked with mentally impaired kids. Also, he and his soon-to-be ex-wife had raised six boys.

Now, he explained, it was time to move on. Time to change. Except where the family was concerned.

"He's doing fine, great," I reassured one of my sisters when she called, as did others throughout that first week, to ask whether Jim was okay. "Why don't you quit asking how he is and just leave him alone?"

"For christsakes, Louie! He's getting a divorce. How okay could he be?"

I paused and took note of a silent anger welling up inside me. I felt like one of those Thanksgiving toms with the plastic thermometer that pops up when it's finished cooking. I purposely hadn't been home for months and months while I attempted to change my life and get a grip on a situation that had spiraled out of control.

Yet suddenly I was back in the fold. Back on the phone, in a conversation that was too familiar, proving to me that a dysfunctional family is stronger than the strongest resolutions. And sneakier than a crooked agent. Dysfunctional families have their own set of booby traps. They lie dormant, quiet, camouflaged. One day they'll send you a basket of fruit, then the next day,—whammo!

I unwrapped a candy bar I had hidden under the placemats I kept on top of the refrigerator.

I hung up and looked around the kitchen. I was starving big time. If I'd been a drug addict, I'd have gotten high immediately. As it was, my mind was like a neon sign flashing a simple message: doughnuts.

Just then, I heard the front door open.

"Jim?"

"Yeah, it's me, Lou," he said. "I stopped by Carl Jr.'s and picked up some dinner."

Oh mercy, I thought. Mercy, mercy, mercy.

HELLO CRUEL WORLD

Watergate

32

The sun was fading. If I craned my neck, I could see most of Madonna's white house perched on the hill, looking like a marshmallow against the backdrop of chocolate-colored hillside and lawn the hue of green frosting. As usual, nothing was going on. If I looked outside without craning my neck, I could see my brother hammering away at the deck.

It was nearly finished.

I was lying on my back in the living room, resting on the floor next to the sofa, throwing pillows at the remote control, which was still on top of the TV. I'd forgotten to get it as I walked by, and now I was comfortable. Isn't that always the way? I wanted to knock it down and then use a big book to drag it along the floor. Heaven forbid I should get up.

"Hey, what are you doing?" my brother asked.

I'd been concentrating so hard. I didn't hear the hammering stop or Jim enter the room.

"Oh, nothing," I lied.

"I thought I saw you throwing something."

"Naw." Then I pointed toward the TV. "Hey, could you get me that remote?"

I flipped through the channels as if they were food coupons in a little box and I was waiting for something to catch my eye. Jim left the room and came back with a soda. He was nearly finished with the deck, he said. Maybe another day's work and then he was heading back to Minneapolis. He wanted to find a job and get on with his life.

"Why don't you come up for a few weeks?" he asked. "Spend some time with the family?"

Family?

I jumped up with a look of terror painted across my face. A shiver of panic shook my body. I grabbed an enormous silver crucifix that I'd found in the bushes beneath Madonna's house and waved it at my brother. I held up a full-length mirror. I quickly paged through my address book and looked for Oliver Stone's home number. My conspiracy theory was right; my family had plotted against me since birth. Perhaps Stone could make a film about it.

Just kidding.

But I did say to my brother, "Go home? Oh man, you've been in the sun too long."

183

HELLO CRUEL WORLD

"What do you mean?" he asked.

• • • • •

First we went outside and surveyed the deck. I didn't know how much I should reveal to Jim. I trusted him as much as I trusted anybody. He'd never done anything to hurt me. Still, I didn't know if I should tell him *everything*.

"Is it your weight?" he said.

I threw a pebble over the railing and watched it disappear in the canyon below us.

"Because you're trying, Lou," he went on. "You're sticking to the salads pretty good. And you're exercising regularly. What more can you do?"

For a moment, I almost told him about my five-year plan for the family. In my head, I had it all worked out. In five years, the entire Anderson clan would be one big happy unit, staging regular get-togethers, singing, traveling, sending mushy Hallmark cards every few weeks. I even envisioned myself in Stockholm, accepting the Nobel Peace Prize.

"I said, 'What more can you do?' "

"Something," I answered.

"What?"

"I can find out why I'm fat. Why food is the only thing in the world that makes me feel good."

"You seeing a shrink?" he asked.

"No. But come look at this."

• • • • •

Jim followed me into the den. I sat him down on the couch and took out several files stuffed with papers.

"What's all that?" he asked.

"I'll tell you in a second," I said. "But first, I want to ask you a question."

"Okay," he said.

"Do you think Mom and Dad loved me?"

"Oh Christ, Louie. Not this shit again. Didn't you already go through this in your book?"

· · · · ·

The biggest problem in a dysfunctional family is that nobody ever talks about the truth. Everybody knows what it is but avoids it like quicksand. After opening the files and spreading the papers in front of my brother, I realized that I was once again stepping into territory considered taboo by my family. Off limits.

"What is all this?" Jim asked uneasily.

"Believe it or not, it's our family history," I said. "A geneology."

"Where'd you get it?"

"Remember my friend Marty?" I asked. "He helped me put it together."

Jim leaned closer. There were papers and pictures, charts and photocopied certificates of births and deaths. Months earlier, Marty had written that there were eight thousand stories in the Anderson family history. As I was rummaging through the piles, it suddenly seemed to me as if there were more. My dad's side was from Norway. Some of them were Vikings. Every generation from the tenth century to the present was alike: They fought and drank. My mom's people were religious fanatics. They sailed to the U.S. on the *Mayflower* and married into a family that had run afoul of the law.

"Interesting," Jim said, trying to find the same meaning **185**

HELLO CRUEL WORLD

that I had. "But so what? What's the point of all this?"

"The point is," I began, then faltered, looking for a way to express what I'd known intuitively but had never, until now, had the evidence to put into words. "The point is that for years and years—for generations, in fact—we've considered ourselves a normal family when, in fact, that's a sham. A lie. And over time, our family has accumulated one lie on top of another."

Suddenly I was pumped up with energy, excitement. I felt like Woodward and Bernstein must have when they were uncovering Watergate. It wasn't that different, either. Watergate involved a crime and a cover-up, and though his subordinates were punished, Nixon was pardoned. That sounded a lot like my dad and our family. However, society was filled with examples like this—poverty, hunger, homelessness, trouble in our schools, racism, the savings-and-loan scandal . . .

We're told it's all normal. Hell, it's sick. We're told the system will take care of it. It doesn't. One lie heaped on top of another. No different from a dysfunctional family. And aren't we all just one big family?

"Finally, I've uncovered what nobody else in the family has wanted to talk about," I said. "I know where the trouble originated. I know the truth."

Jim raised his eyebrows. "Congrats. But what are you going to do with the truth?"

I was silent.

Completely stumped. Marty had done great work digging up all the information about my ancestry. I'd struggled long and hard to make sense out of it. My origins. My roots. But now that I had it, I didn't know what to do with it.

What had I thought would happen?

I didn't know.

So I didn't have an answer for Jim.

"Maybe nobody cares," he said. "Maybe you should just drop it and let things be."

Gustav Stickley

33

My sixth sense was acting up again. Fine-tuned, you might say. Which meant that the mother ship must have been hovering close by. Because from the moment I woke up, I knew that the day was going to unfold differently than I'd planned.

Several weeks earlier, I'd planned to go shopping for some craftsman furniture with my friend Bob. He picked me up at eleven. We were at the flea market in Pasadena by noon. My pockets were filled with checks and cash, and I had the enormous outdoor market cased in a few minutes.

Under normal circumstances, I would've been poised for a big, expensive purchase, indulging the giddiness that comes with a bargain and a new addition to my collection of priceless thingamajigs.

Under normal circumstances, I showed up at these flea markets and thought, Okay, what's for sale? What could make me feel better? Whatever problem I had, I knew I had two options: eat or buy something. Usually I did both. But sometimes a good purchase was enough to get me by. Like a stick of chewing gum when you really want a burger. A quick fix.

That's how I ended up with my car—even though I could've bought a farm for the same price. That's also how I began amassing my collection of craftsman furniture. Prior to that, I'd been into Southwestern. Then somebody at one of these orgies for compulsive shoppers asked me if I'd ever heard of Gustav Stickley. I hadn't.

"You're in show business, aren't you?" she asked.

"Yeah."

"Spielberg's into Stickley. Everybody's into Stickley. You should get into Stickley."

"Okay. Get me into Stickley."

"What kind of Stickley do you want? Chair? Table? Couch? End tables?"

"What kind should I get?"

"Everybody's getting everything."

"Okay. Get me everything. But how much will it cost?"

"Prices are only going up."

"Then, Christ, hurry up!"

• • • • •

Bob spotted a chair and called me over. I nodded, made **189**

H E L L O   C R U E L   W O R L D

190 some noises, and walked off. Bob followed. I told him to offer several thousand. No more than three grand. It was worth about seven. I got it for twenty-five hundred.

Ordinarily, I would've been ecstatic. But this time something was wrong. I was like a hunter who'd suddenly lost his taste for meat. It was as if Wolfgang Puck woke up one morning and hated pizza. Victory left me unimpressed. All I thought about was that I had no room for it.

By the time I got home, I couldn't stand the chair. There really *wasn't* room for it. And on top of that, I hated myself for buying it. It was the same feeling I had after eating junk food late at night.

Nevertheless, I tried it in a few places. The chair didn't look right anywhere. There was just no room for it.

My house and everything in it had been like one big Snickers bar to me. Delicious and comforting. Suddenly, though, it was all making me sick.

In a fit of disgust, I opened the hall closet and tried to jam my new twenty-five-hundred-dollar craftsman chair inside. There wasn't any room there either. Something was blocking it. I looked in to see what the obstacle was and saw a box on the floor. I tried pushing it farther back, but it wouldn't go any further.

I scooted it out with my foot, pushed the chair into the closet, and slammed the door shut.

I didn't want that chair anymore.

Then when I turned around and faced the living room full of craftsman furniture, more than one hundred thousand dollars' worth, I suddenly didn't want any of it anymore. Not a single piece of Stickley, no matter what its value. At that moment, I discovered that when something loses its meaning, its value can be a million dollars and it doesn't matter a bit.

It's just stuff.

· · · · ·

And so it became stuff that I decided to get rid of. Not really get rid of. I wasn't up to a clean break from my possessions, from the things that had defined my material life for so long.

I just needed a rest from them. A break. What an attorney would call a trial separation.

I rented storage space in an industrial building in the middle of Hollywood. God only knew what secrets were locked inside that building. Secrets and problems. I myself had leased three enormous rooms for my stuff. One for things from the past. These were artifacts I could never part with and things I couldn't even remember getting. Then one for things from the present, things ranging from photographs to my Stickley furniture. And then one empty room. Really. An empty room. This was for the stuff that I didn't even have yet, stuff that hadn't even crossed my eye, but stuff that I knew my compulsive need to waste good money would one day *need*.

A friend of mine allowed me to talk him into packing the stuff in boxes, labeling them, and then hauling the whole shebang to the storage facility, which would send me a bill each month reminding me that I still had a life somewhere.

I knew that eventually I'd have to face that stuff down and sort it out. Wasn't that what I was trying to do anyway? Sort everything out?

· · · · ·

The house was empty after that. But not empty enough, **191**

192   it turned out.

The same night everything was carted away I was lolling on my bed, watching a movie and waiting for something to jolt me out of my lethargy. I wanted something to happen. I was looking for a sign.

As in the movies, it came in a most obvious form, which I, of course, didn't recognize at first. The telephone rang.

The house was dark as I hurried down the hallway, toward the kitchen so I could listen to the answering machine and hear who was calling me. God forbid I should pick up the telephone. Halfway there, in front of the closet where I'd put the chair, I hit my foot on something.

"Ooooouuuuuu!" I yowled.

I did that pain dance everybody does.

"Who the hell put that there?" I said out loud even though no one else was there.

I thought about looking down, then decided not to. The toe might be gone. I flipped on the light and looked down anyway. No, I hadn't run into a frozen turkey. It wasn't even a stale Ding-Dong.

It was a box.

A simple box wrapped in brown paper. Then I remembered. It was my mom's box. I'd forgotten about it. I wondered why it hadn't been put into storage with the others. I thought it ingenious that it had managed to follow me around. I pulled out the note in the envelope attached to the top.

"Dear Louie," it began. "Here are some things of mom's that we thought you might like."

• • • • •

As I debated whether to open the box, I imagined what

might be inside. The possibilities were limitless—a pressure cooker, an old shoe, electrical cords, a clock, old report cards, canned goods.

Did it even matter?

Thinking about this raised an interesting question about the issues I'd been trying to deal with in my life. If my mom's life could be fit into a little box, what the hell was I doing with a houseful of stuff? Stuff that I didn't even like? I would've traded everything I owned in a flash, without one thought, simply to have my mom alive. If only for a moment.

If only long enough to ask her if I'd been wanted. To ask her if she'd loved me.

To tell her that I loved her.

• • • • •

I shook the box once more before deciding not to open it and putting it on the floor in the pantry.

It had been sixteen hours since I woke up, sensing a change. As was often the case, I'd been right. Sitting in the semidarkness of a living room that was still chock-full of museum-quality furniture in addition to what I'd put in storage, I listened to my heart beat in the quiet of my empty home. I heard the sound of church bells in the quiet of perfect solitude. Somehow, sometime, during the day, I knew that I'd changed—or was on the verge of it—and that from now on, my life would be different.

No Crosses Counted

3
4

I was at home. It was late. And I was by myself. Tossing and turning in bed, I was unable to find a comfortable position, feeling as if someone was jabbing me with elbows and knees. Actually, I felt as if there was a foot against the back of my neck and that someone was demanding, "Change."

"All right," I replied. "Let me up."

Of course, I was thinking, My fingers are crossed. I'm not changing.

"I don't believe you, Louie!"

194 "No crosses counted," I pleaded. "I'll change. Really, I will."

• • • • •

Which is how I arrived at this crucial conclusion. Diet and exercise can only get you so far in the struggle to drop excessive poundage. The most crucial as well as the most difficult part of losing weight is this question: Do you want to stop killing yourself? Do you want to change?

If the answer's yes, then there's no way to avoid the fact that change will result in the very thing you're trying to avoid:

Pain.

Losing weight, I realized, is like removing a tattoo. It's going to hurt like hell. If I was finally going to be successful, I had to admit the pain. Accept that it was going to hurt. In every previous diet I'd attempted, throughout my entire life, the only aspect I wasn't willing to deal with was the pain of change. I'd had enough pain in my life. I didn't want to change.

Like any abused child, I grew up trying to deny everything that had happened to me. I tried never to admit the truth. I spent my life trying to make up for the loss of love, overcompensating for the hurt I suffered, for my lack of self-esteem and self-worth.

I couldn't change my family. I couldn't go back and repair everything, make everything nice.

In all honesty, I was as guilty for trying to change them as they were for trying to change me.

It was a standoff.

I didn't have to forget the past. I couldn't forget it. No way.

However, there was something I could do. I could forgive. **195**

196 I could forgive everyone—my mom and dad, my brothers and sisters. The Vikings. The Pilgrims. Every person who ever did me wrong.

I could also take responsibility for my actions. Something few people endeavor.

And then I could get on with my life.

And then, and only then, I could stop trying to kill myself.

• • • • •

That type of life change doesn't happen overnight, but that didn't stop me from trying. Shortly past eleven, I called an acquaintance who'd once mentioned that he knew a real estate agent. I called the number he gave me, and the moment the realtor answered, I knew I'd woken her up. I said I wanted to put my house up for sale.

She sounded more tired than enthused and mentioned that her office was listed in the Beverly Hills phone book.

"By the way," she said. "How much do you want to list your home for?"

"Around a million six," I said.

At that moment, I made a new best friend.

"When can I see it?" she asked, suddenly wide awake. "Just let me get my book."

• • • • •

After the call, I took a final, sentimental stroll through my house. I was going to get rid of everything. Stickley furniture included. I wasn't going to insulate myself any longer. I wasn't going to put up barriers. Not with material possessions. Not with food. I was going to sell it all and lose it all and take the scary plunge into the world.

I ended up standing on the deck outside with a can of diet soda in my hand. The night sky was clear, and there were stars glistening overhead, a rare event in L.A. When I looked up the hill, I saw an even rarer event. There was actually something going on at Madonna's house. Probably a sex party. Then again, maybe not. The lights were on. Of course . . .

At any rate, I saw people in every window, people walking around and talking, people leaning over the railing in her backyard. And then I saw someone stand up on the wall and hold a glass up.

"Hello!" he yelled into the dark canyon, though it might as well have been directly to me. "Hello, out there! Hello, cruel world!"

HELLO CRUEL WORLD

A Cool Million

35

Fate has a cruel sense of humor. The next morning I got a call from my agent, who'd received a serious offer from one of the networks for me to do a half-hour sitcom. The producers and writers were top notch. The network was guaranteeing twelve episodes. The money they were talking about was too disgusting to mention. The weekly pay alone was more than most families bring in during an entire year.

Talk about temptation. It was a dream come true.

"What do you say, Lou?" he asked.

"You're going to kill me," I said.

"You want more money? I think I can get them to pump in an extra ten grand a week."

"You're still going to kill me."

"What's the matter?" Now he sounded worried. "If it's not money, what is it?"

"I'm getting out of the business for a while," I answered in a serious tone he didn't recognize.

"Lou," he said. "Am I hearing you right? You're quitting?"

"Temporarily. Yeah."

"Are you nuts?"

"Maybe. But I put my house up for sale, and as soon as it sells I'm leaving town."

There was a long pause. The quiet was unsettling.

"Lou, what the hell's going on here?"

"I'm changing my life," I said. "I'm getting healthy. If I don't, my career won't matter. 'Cause I'll be dead."

"I can still book you." He chuckled lightly. "Hey, just joking. Seriously, Lou, listen to me."

I heard him. He didn't want me to change. And I knew why. It upset his life. That's why people don't like you to change. That's part of the pressure on you when you try to change.

"Have a cup of coffee," he continued. "Then go over to the Farmer's Market. Get yourself a nice, big breakfast. A few sweet rolls, some eggs and bacon and hash browns. Then give me a ring, and we'll talk."

I felt like giving him John Belushi's old agent's number.

"Sorry," I said. "My mind's made up."

$\bullet\ \bullet\ \bullet\ \bullet\ \bullet$

It wasn't easy to turn down a series. It would've been hard **199**

HELLO CRUEL WORLD

200 for anybody to walk away from more than one million dollars a year, but when you've grown up as poor as I did, it's even harder. All you think about is that figure. One million. It's got a great sound to it. One million. All you can see is an endless stream of zeros, except that somewhere at the head of the pack is a one.

One million dollars.

Believe me, it hurt.

But I'd already learned that money didn't make me happy.

God knows, I tried to let it. I spent generously. I bought everything I wanted. I never said no. I had an equation in my head:

· · · · ·

Money   Happiness
Lots of Money   Lots of Happiness

· · · · ·

But it was a lot like algebra or geometry.

I didn't get it.

It didn't work for me.

· · · · ·

Most people wouldn't buy that for a second. They wouldn't hear a word past a million dollars. They'd drift off into space and think, "What would I do if I had a million dollars?" Most people would do the following:

a) Take care of their parents
b) Buy a new car
c) Pay off the house

d) Splurge on something they didn't need

e) Help the homeless

Okay, scratch that last one. But that's about it. And then they'd find themselves asking, "Is that all there is to one million dollars? What else can I do? What else can I buy? What else will make me happy?"

It sounds cliché, but money doesn't help in the areas that count most. Health. Family. Friends. And love.

$$\bullet \ \bullet \ \bullet \ \bullet \ \bullet$$

My realtor was someone who wouldn't have understood what I was doing.

I'd been busy. Nearly all of my furniture and stuff was already sold, donated, or in storage when she arrived. Except for my treadmill and stereo. I was zeroing in on two miles and listening to Prince when she rang the doorbell and let herself in before I could make the first move toward the door.

She waved, and then gave the place a once-over so calculating it would've made a burglar jealous.

"Do you have another bathroom and bedroom that I don't see?" she asked.

"No."

"Too bad." She shook her head. "That's too bad."

"Why's it too bad? When I bought the house, I was told that I didn't need any more rooms."

"Well," she said, walking and looking and letting me follow, "the market changes."

$$\bullet \ \bullet \ \bullet \ \bullet \ \bullet$$

I didn't understand about how this real estate thing op- **201**

202 erated. The way I saw it, selling my house was about one notch more enjoyable than buying a used car.

For starters, I didn't get the six percent commission thing my realtor explained to me. Was that an arbitrary figure? And then I didn't understand why the market was always bad. She groaned that it was in the pits, but hadn't it been down the toilet several years earlier when I'd bought the house? And finally, I didn't see why I had to leave whenever she wanted to show the house.

"Well, it's not good to have the owner here," she insisted.

"Why not?" I argued. "I can tell them the things that are wrong and the things that are good."

"I can do that, too."

"But you're lying to them."

"Don't insult me. I earn my commission."

"See! You just did it again. Another lie!"

• • • • •

No matter what happened, the realtor never once allowed her smile to fade. She was always charming to me. Until one cool, fateful evening. The evening she called up with an offer. Before she told me what it was, she prepared me for disappointment by calling me a thief.

"They think you're listing it too high," she said.

"But you talked to me about comps, what all the other homes in the neighborhood have sold for lately. You're the one who said list it where it's at."

"Well, the market changed."

• • • • •

When she told me the offer, which was over two hundred

thousand less than I'd paid for the house, I reacted the way any self-respecting seller would. I got spiteful. I thought, "Well, I'll keep it then. I'm going down with my house."

Later, I found myself thinking about a fire. Maybe I'd just burn it down. I started walking around the empty house, grumbling, "That's what I'm gonna do. I'm gonna burn the son-of-a-bitch down."

Of course I didn't.

But I was mad. I felt cheated. What was this realtor doing besides advertising in the paper and escorting stooges through my house? I could've done that. But then we reached that closing stuff, and I saw the light. I could do heart surgery before I could understand all the closing instructions. I asked one question during escrow and got an explanation that lasted for thirty minutes. I nodded, looked interested, and when it was finally my turn to speak I threw my cards on the table.

"Oh, I get it," I said, giving up. "Where do I sign?"

• • • • •

"Congratulations, Mr. Anderson," my realtor said as soon as we got outside. "You just sold your house for one million dollars."

I smiled.

"Think about it," she said, so happy that she was barely able to stop herself from drooling on the sidewalk. "One million dollars. One million dollars! Let me say it again. One million dollars. That's a lot of money."

What neither of us mentioned was that I'd bought the house for one million two hundred thousand and change. I'd sold it for a million. Despite the realtor's enthusiasm, I'd taken a loss of more than two hundred thousand dollars.

203

204   If only I'd lost that many calories.

"What am I going to do with a million dollars?" I asked in a tone that didn't beg for an answer.

One came anyway.

"I can show you a house," she smiled. "Of course it's not as nice as your old house. The market's changed . . ."

If there's a hell, I thought, she's going there. Realtor's hell. It's one big open house. No doors. No buyers. Everyone just walks around, exchanging business cards and complaining that the market stinks.

"No thanks," I said. "I'm not really interested."

Forgiveness

3
6

Without a home of my own, I checked into a hotel at the beach and fell into a peaceful routine of doing nothing. I read and walked. I didn't have a telephone. I unplugged the television. The time passed without my noticing. My childhood train whistled. It slowed. And then it chugged by without stopping.

I felt no need to get on. I ate when I was hungry and most of the food I ate was healthy.

I felt good and calm.

206   Until the episode with the bird.

• • • • •

Driving home after seeing a late afternoon movie, I mar-
veled at the colors of the sunset. Brilliant shades of red, pink,
and orange, mingled with dark purple clouds, hung over the
Pacific. It looked like Hawaii was on fire. Bobby McFerrin's
song "Don't Worry, Be Happy" blasted from the radio. I
trained my eyes on the traffic ahead of me. The windows were
rolled down. I enjoyed the refreshing coolness of the night
air. I actually let thoughts of my family creep into my con-
sciousness. I thought about calling them. Maybe even going
home. I kinda missed those guys. That's how good I felt.

Then I heard a noise.

Frruuuump! Pooooom! Puuuuufffff! Whooooop!

What the hell was that?

I looked in the rearview mirror, and there it was. A jumble
of feathers rolling and blowing.

A bird. I hit a bird.

• • • • •

He was doing that one-wing thing, trying to get out of the
road. I felt bad. Sort of.

"Stupid goddamned bird," I yelled out the window, sounding like my dad. "You should've been flying. What the hell
were you doing walking in the middle of the goddamned
road? The street is for cars. Christ, there should be warning
signs, 'Watch out for strolling birds!'"

• • • • •

I didn't think the incident would affect me as much as it

did. After all, where I come from people hit deer all the time. There are lots of deer on the road. It's a regional hazard. Comes with the territory. They just stand there, staring as you barrel down the highway.

Ever wonder what they're thinking?

Is that a Toyota? Or is tonight my lucky night and those are two motorcycles?

· · · · ·

I felt the old anxiety start creeping back, that unsettled, clawing feeling at the pit of my stomach, empty and churning acidic juices that wanted to be mopped up by meatball sandwiches and oatmeal cookies. I began hearing the familiar whistle of that old train coming around distant curves, getting closer and closer. And I became obsessed by the idea of heaven and hell.

Was I going to hell for killing that bird?

Hitler, Saddam Hussein, and Louie in the same hell? Because if that was true, then I needed to cause more trouble.

There must be subchambers in hell, I reasoned. Different levels. Rooms at street level. Rooms with air conditioners. Rooms with a view of the inferno. Rooms where they automatically bring ketchup when you order fries.

How bad, I wondered, do you have to be before they come and take you away to hell? Maybe there's a bargaining period. I could talk to those little guys. I could promise to do volunteer work. I could . . .

· · · · ·

"I could forgive you," the priest said. "Would that make you feel better?"

207

H E L L O   C R U E L   W O R L D

208

We'd been in line at the Department of Motor Vehicles. Both of us were renewing our licenses. The priest looked like a character actor whose face I'd seen a thousand times in Westerns but whose name I couldn't recall. I avoided eye contact until the priest smiled and asked if I was Louie Anderson the comedian.

"Yes," I said.

"You're very funny," he said.

"Thanks," I smiled. "But I killed a bird last week."

I don't know why I said that. It just came out. My first confession in . . . probably ever. He seemed perplexed. I told him the story of how I'd hit the bird and driven away without stopping, without even leaving a note on the bird's beak.

"Perhaps you should drive more carefully," he suggested.

"I'll try. But I don't want to go to hell just for that one little thing."

I noticed a twinkle of light in the priest's eyes. He seemed to be holding back a laugh. That's when he first mentioned the notion of forgiveness. He could forgive me, if I wanted him to. Did I WANT him to? That was like asking, "Did I want to spend eternity like a pig on a skewer, the main course at Satan's luau, hanging over humanity's largest barbeque?"

"And that's it?" I asked. "You forgive me and I get to live my life?"

"If you let yourself," he said. "See, it's not really I who forgives you."

"It's not?"

"No," he said. "It's all up to you. You have to forgive yourself."

As those words of wisdom began to sink into my thick head, I heard the lady behind the counter call for the next in line, after which the priest stepped forward and I never saw or spoke to him again.

• • • • •

But that night something strange happened. Well, something even stranger.

For some reason I couldn't get comfortable in bed. I called housekeeping and requested five new pillows be sent up. Then, without having thought about it, without ever having made such a request before, I asked for something else:

A pad of paper and a pen.

"Right away, Mr. Anderson," the woman said.

• • • • •

Paper. Pen.

Why?

I shrugged. The idea had popped into my mind the way the urge for a Snickers bar used to just appear. There was no explaining it. It simply was. I just had to wait for the stuff to arrive and then see what happened.

• • • • •

Two hours later I finished writing the last of ten letters to my brothers and sisters. I sent them the following morning. My decision to write them was purely emotional. If I'd thought about it, analyzed it, I don't know if I would've written any of those letters. But as soon as the paper and pen had been delivered, I began writing and didn't quit until I'd "spoken" to each and every one of them.

In each one, I'd simply asked if there was anything I could do for them.

209

HELLO CRUEL WORLD

"What do you want? Can I help with anything?"

It was a risk. A definite risk. But what the hell. Why not, I told myself, open your heart as wide as you've opened your checkbook and see what happens?

As the priest said, "It's all up to you."

• • • • •

And really, the more I thought about it, the more I realized it was worth the one hundred thousand dollars I'd given and loaned over the years to have gotten to know my brothers and sisters better. I felt as if I finally understood who they were and what they were about. That understanding is exactly what I needed to rise above the fray that had always defined my familial relationships. The more I knew about my family, the more aware I became of myself.

The more I loved myself, the more I could love my family, my brothers and sisters.

I was learning. Growing in the right way.

Possessions didn't matter. Neither did money. People were what mattered.

People and family.

• • • • •

After dropping the letters in the mailbox, I felt cleansed and somehow fulfilled. Yet the day had only begun and I didn't have much of anything else planned. I ended up on the bench outside my hotel and spent the afternoon thinking about the events of the past few days.

"It's all up to you. You have to forgive yourself."

I'd already forgiven everyone in my family. My dad, my mom, everyone.

Finally, it was my turn.

211

Goodbye Jumbo

3
7

One of the benefits of living at the beach was keeping the windows of my hotel room wide open every night, allowing the ocean breeze to wrap around me like a baby blanket. For the first time in ages, I was sleeping soundly.

I had also begun to dream again.

Night after night. I actually looked forward to my dreams. To sifting through the wreckage of my life.

To rebuilding.

· · · · ·

In these dreams the dust around me began to settle. I recognized shapes and places I hadn't been able to make out before. I confronted the fears that had previously caused me to run. I faced the emotions that had inspired and then sustained this journey of self-discovery and self-forgiveness.

• • • • •

I was waiting in the fog. Waiting for a long time. As the fog lifted, I found myself on a platform, standing alone, a ticket in hand. It was dated March 23, 1954—my birthday. The destination read, "End of the line." The ticket's expiration: "Whenever you decide." The fare was the same: "Whatever you're willing to pay."

Shortly afterward, a train came to a stop in front of me. A long, ten-car train pulled—no, not by a big steam engine —but a shiny, new Bonneville. It rested on steel train wheels instead of white walls. The engineer turned his head slightly, glancing over his shoulder to see if I was getting on. I saw a hand-rolled cigarette hanging from his lower lip exactly as it had from my dad's. Then he turned away and tipped a can of beer to his mouth.

"All aboard!" a voice from the back shouted.

Then the clang of a bell, the hissing of the engine trading its reluctant idle for a measured chug.

"All aboard!"

• • • • •

My train car seemed fancy. As the train began to move, I stuck my head out the window. The outside of the car was painted like a circus wagon. There was writing on the side. In bold letters, it said, "LOUIE—The World's Biggest Co-

213

214 median."

I wanted to get off, but there was no getting off. The only exit was into another car.

The first signal I had were the cats. Not just the circus master's pet tabby, who was no friend of the mice I entertained during off hours, but the lions and tigers, too. Their nervousness had reached a new pitch. Now they were pacing and growling hysterically. The poodles were yapping. The horses had come unglued (some gallows humor), and the giraffe, whose long neck and head poked through the roof of his boxcar so that he alone could see ahead, was stomping anxiously.

"See anything?" I called to him, my trunk sticking out the window of my private car. "What's going on out there?"

The next car was empty, although it was decorated with things that were familiar to me. Personal items. Pictures of me on stage in Las Vegas. With Johnny Carson. With Eddie Murphy and Arsenio. Rosanne Barr and me on our Vast Waistland Tour. Another wall was filled with family photos, pictures all in a row of Roger, Kent, Rhea, Mary, Jim, Shanna, Bill, Sheila, Lisa. There was a blank spot. Then came one of Tommy. On top of this brood was a photo of Mom and Dad.

Where was I in all of this? Where was I?

Just then a man entered the car, startling me from the cloud of confusion. I saw he was the conductor. His nameplate read "Kunze," my high-school gym teacher come back to haunt me one more time. He asked for my ticket and punched it a number of times. When he handed it back, I saw that he had punched out the words "Face the music, fat boy."

The first sign that the animals' sense of foreboding was justified had come a few minutes earlier. The train jerked, slowed down, then all of a sudden picked up speed again. Instead of the rhythmic chug-a-chug-a-chug the train engine normally made, though, we were engulfed by a terrible rumbling noise unlike anything I'd ever heard, more frightening than the noise made by a herd of stampeding elephants. The faster the train sped, the louder the noise grew and the more scared I became.

"Curve coming up," the giraffe yelled down to me. "Better hold on."

The scenery outside was familiar. The woods near my old house in the projects. Ames Elementary School and its jungle gym. Mrs. Ogden, the teacher with the rolled-down socks, waving to the kids, and the fattest girl in school eating an ice cream cone that was dripping onto her shoes, the tears falling from her eyes as fast as the ice cream was from her cone. The storekeeper from whom I used to buy Red Hots.

I waved to everyone, but they didn't seem to see me, and the train picked up speed.

215

HELLO CRUEL WORLD

216

Word spread that the brakes were gone. There was no way for us to slow down. The train was out of control.

I trumpeted. The other animals whimpered and hollered for help. I saw one of the clowns jump from his car and roll down the dirt embankment. Then another. And another. They were followed by a half-dozen poodles who were part of their act. All were still in costume.

There was an open door. I heard water running and peeked inside. A bathroom. It smelled of the perfume that my mom dabbed behind her ears. I stepped inside, expecting to see her. All I found was a picture of her on the wall, the one of us together. Mom and me. Me leaning on her shoulder. Her smiling that smile that made me feel like a million dollars.

It was the picture that showed how closely I resembled her.

I touched my finger to my lips and blew her a kiss.

· · · · ·

Entering the adjoining car, I was struck by the beauty and elegance of its decor. Everything was clean and bright and placed exactly where it ought to be. My sister Lisa was standing beside a table, arranging a bouquet of flowers in a vase.

"Hi, Lisa," I said.

She turned, and there were tears in her eyes, a look of anger and frustration on her face.

"What's wrong?" I asked.

She nodded to the flowers, which on closer inspection weren't flowers at all. They were long green stems topped by photographs of everyone in our family. Mom and Dad and all eleven of us kids.

"Louie, I can't get these to look right," Lisa wailed.

I took the stems from her and stuck them in the vase just as they were.

"And you never will," I said. "You just have to accept them as they are."

"How do you know?"

"I just do," I said. "I figured it out."

• • • • •

"Where are we going?" Lisa asked as I took her hand and led her into yet another car.

This one was a mess. We made our way carefully, until we spotted Shanna sorting through the junk. She looked up, surprised.

"Oh, there you are, Louie," she said. "I was afraid I might not find you."

She got up and hugged me, and soon the three of us, Lisa, Shanna, and me, were standing in the middle of the car as the train sped down the tracks, hugging one another as we hadn't in years. Maybe as we hadn't ever before.

Just then Kent burst in the door. Out of breath, my brother was followed by my other brothers and sisters. All of them except for Billy, who has been homeless and out of touch for longer than any of us feel comfortable remembering. For the first time since Mom's funeral, we were together.

A family.

217

HELLO CRUEL WORLD

"Train's going to crash!" Kent said excitedly. "It's going to crash!"

"What are we going to do?" Tommy, the youngest, asked.

· · · · ·

Then I felt it. The burn of everyone staring at me, looking to me for an answer.

For some reason I was perfectly calm. I even smiled. Then I moved to the door and opened it. The wind roared in. The sound was deafening. I looked at the ground speeding by beneath the train's wheels. Then I looked back at my family.

I still wasn't scared. I knew what to tell them. I had the plan.

"Jump!" I yelled above the din. "Let's get off this goddamned train!"

Then the train hit a curve, and I felt a strange, massive pull that I was unable to resist. The floor went out from under my feet and I tumbled violently onto the embankment, hitting my head on the hard ground. My eyes glazed and blurred. A pain unlike anything I'd ever experienced consumed me till I went limp and lost my bearings completely. I pictured myself lying on the ground, helpless, in a gray heap, like the elephants I'd left behind as a child in Africa.

"There's another train up there!" I heard a panic-stricken voice cry out.

This was followed by a tremendous explosion.

It sounded like the end of the world.

The first thing I realized was that I'd survived the fall from the train. Next, that I'd also survived the explosion and ensuing fireball. My eyes opened and I saw the blue sky. Then trees. Then grass. When the world righted itself, I saw my brothers and sisters brushing themselves off. Everyone was okay.

Almost.

In the distance was a band of light. As my vision returned, it got brighter and brighter.

Silhouetted against the glow, I saw my mother in the jungle. She was walking. I called out to her. Mom! I didn't hear a reply, but she stopped and turned her head toward me, motioning me to follow. I hurried.

"He's dead," I heard someone say.

"Get away from him, Louie," said an older fellow in the crowd of onlookers.

"The wreck must've killed him," said the boy, who gently put his hand on the side of my trunk.

The little boy was wearing overalls and a baseball cap. A reed of tasty straw protruded from his mouth. He must've picked it up from one of the cages. I'd enjoyed eating straw, too. He patted my head. The others were calling to him. He motioned for them to go on without him, then stroked my head several more times.

"Goodbye," he whispered. "Goodbye, Jumbo."

219

H E L L O   C R U E L   W O R L D

220

Hello Cruel World

3
8

I looked over at the clock. Five-thirty A.M.

How long had I been lying in bed, staring into the darkness and listening to the waves breaking on the shore outside the windows of my room? Did it matter?

For the first time in weeks I hadn't slept well. The dreams that had possessed me, that I had looked forward to watching as much as any movie, evaporated with my ability to put together six or seven hours of decent shut-eye.

What was going on?

I looked at the clock again. Five-thirty-two A.M.

221

222   I'd read books. I'd listened to books on tape. I'd tuned into talk radio and heard that that Big One could happen momentarily, the experts advising everyone to have at least seventy-two hours' worth of emergency provisions, including water and canned goods. I had nothing.

I'd counted sheep, goats, elephants, and family members all night long.

Now what?

· · · · ·

The first thought that popped into my head was predictable.

Doughnuts.

Glazed. Chocolate. Buttermilk.

Hot and sweet.

With milk.

Ah.

· · · · ·

Then I thought of something else.

McDonald's.

Two of those egg, bacon, and cheese biscuits would put me to sleep.

Nothing like a little grease to end the day. Or to start it.

· · · · ·

But what I really felt like was melon.

A big boat of sliced cantaloupe. Melon drowning in juice and natural sugar.

· · · · ·

What was going on?

* * * * *

The answer became apparent as I got dressed. Over the past few weeks I'd lost around twenty pounds, and without trying. I simply ate healthy foods and only when I was hungry rather than all the time. The weight disappeared on its own, and at its own pace.

What was going on?

Easy.

I just didn't need the fat anymore.

* * * * *

It was close to six.

I got in my car and drove through quiet neighborhoods that were starting to wake up. Automatic sprinkler systems were watering lush lawns as well as the morning *L.A. Times*. Fit men and women were jogging, reminding me of what else I had to begin doing.

It's a cruel world.

Turning onto a busier street, I narrowly missed being mowed down by a city bus whose driver was powering down the straightaway of a thirty-mile-per-hour street at close to fifty, getting his fun before he entered a day of gridlock. I understood, though right after he passed me a bicyclist gave him the finger.

It takes all kinds, I guess.

The windows were down, the radio was up, and the roads were wide open. It was going to be a scorcher out. Very hot. But at the moment the sky was blue. Palm trees reached toward the heaven like towering feather dusters. I realized that **223**

224 L.A. was a pretty nice place when you took away the crowds, smog, earthquakes, crack, gangs, drive-by shootings, freeway shootings, renegade police . . .

• • • • •

I ended up at the grocery store.

Walking into a fully stocked, well-lit grocery store has to be one of life's thrills. It is for me. There are so many possibilities. So many taste sensations. So many treats. So many temptations. So many things to choose from.

Potato chips. Nachos. Ice cream. Microwaveable burgers and fries. Spaghetti in a can. Soda.

I passed by the deli and the bakery sections and sensed the saliva building on my tongue. An alarm in my stomach. The folks who design grocery stores are tricky. There's something enticing at every corner.

"Willpower," I told myself. "Willpower."

With my eyes trained straight in front of me and my hands on the cart, I pushed ahead, stopping only when I turned a corner too quickly and nearly ran head-on into an overweight lady with flaming red hair who was pushing her cart with her stomach while she tore into a bag of double-stuff Oreos. My first reaction was, "Hey, watch it," but then I spotted the cookies and the old Louie understood and thought, "Hmmm, breakfast."

"Excuse me," I said.

She gave me one of those raised-eyebrow looks that said, "I see you and I hear you, but I ain't stopping." Then she whipped around the corner and disappeared down the potato chip aisle in search of a second course. I laughed to myself, perhaps nervously, though I knew that what this fat woman was doing to herself wasn't so much funny as much as it was very, very sad.

I should've grabbed her, or blocked her path, and asked the question every fat person refuses to ask herself.

Why are you fat?

Why are you killing yourself?

· · · · ·

We don't ask, because we know the answer.

We know that we don't love ourselves enough to quit.

· · · · ·

I should've stood in her way and shouted the one word that no one close to her dared utter.

STOP!

I should've said, "Get a grip!"

· · · · ·

Admit the truth. Face the facts. The facts of your life.

· · · · ·

I didn't do any of those things. I watched her for a minute as she debated between barbecue and sour-cream-'n'-onion–flavored potato chips. It was a hard choice, made even harder since they'd recently added salt 'n' vinegar and mesquite flavors to the shelves.

"Do you love yourself, Louie?" I asked myself.

"I'm trying," I answered. "I'm really trying."

I trundled forward and arrived at the produce section guilt-free. While my brain feasted on chips, cookies, and pound cake, my eyes zeroed in on giant red tomatoes, celery, **225** yellow bell peppers, hard red apples, bunches of delicious purple and green grapes, palm-sized plums, grapefruits, and, finally, melons.

Honeydew, cranshaw, and cantaloupe.

"It's getting easier," I told myself as I filled bags with fresh fruit.

· · · · ·

"Eight-sixteen," said the checker, a pretty black woman, without looking up, her mind elsewhere.

"Paper or plastic?" the bagger asked.

Christ, I thought, let me out of here. This is way too much pressure for so early in the day.

"Both," I answered. "Paper in plastic."

I wanted to hang around and see what the fat woman bought—probably a six-pack of Diet Coke and some frozen low-cal dinners, along with the Oreos, of course. She wouldn't want anybody to know her secret. I knew, though. I felt guilty about not saying anything to her.

· · · · ·

After fighting morning rush-hour traffic, I returned to the hotel, dumped the fruit into the kitchen sink, and turned on the tap. My mom used to do that, even before we knew that everything—even the freshest fruits—was contaminated by pesticides. The sound of the water running over the produce always seemed to relax her. I found it had the same effect on me.

· · · · ·

I made coffee and ate breakfast. Afterward, I took a long

walk on the beach, then sat on a bench and read the news-paper. The good news was that the Minnesota Twins were still in first place. The bad news? Everything else.

I dumped the paper in a trashcan, but just as I began walking away, something caught my eye. At the bottom of the Classified section, which was folded on top, I spied an ad for a self-storage building. Free Storage. That was a deal. Anything free was a deal.

But looking more closely at the ad, I noticed that building was the same storage place where I had my stuff.

A bell went off in my head.

It was time to deal with the last bit of business in the healing process.

· · · · ·

As I said before:
If you heal the inside, the outside will follow.
I was nearly there.

· · · · ·

I had to wait for a beat-up old Chevy to back out of the driveway before I could pull into the building's parking lot. The driver, a long-haired guy who appeared to be in his early twenties, jumped out, waved, and pushed the heap to the curb, where hideous-smelling gray smoke began billowing from the engine. He lit a cigarette and watched the fiasco with passive disgust. Then it was my turn to pull in and hope for better luck.

"You're up early," said the attendant at the loading dock.
"Yeah," I said, nodding.
"You gonna be long?" he asked.

227

H E L L O   C R U E L   W O R L D

I shrugged. "Don't know."

I stepped into the elevator and rode to the sixth floor. I could barely remember what I had stored in the three enormous rooms that I rented. The walls of the corridor were blank. The cement floor was littered with cigarette butts. I fished for the keys, unlocked the door, and flipped on the light.

Staring me in the face was a mountain of boxes and furniture and assorted things that defied classification.

"How the hell," I said and then silently mouthed the rest of my thought, "did I accumulate so much garbage?"

I kicked a few of the boxes, wondering what I should do with all of this stuff. I didn't have a house to put it in. And I didn't plan on buying a house anytime soon. I walked into the two other rooms, looking and kicking and scratching my head. Then it dawned on me.

Not only didn't I know what was in most of these boxes, but I'd been doing just fine without it.

I decided not to put off what seemed so obvious. I decided to get rid of it.

• • • • •

Why not?

I'd gotten rid of my pain.

I'd gotten rid of my fat. At least I was in the process of doing that.

And now it was time to rid myself of the trappings of a past I no longer needed.

This is what I had feared so much? I laughed.

• • • • •

About an hour later the sweat was pouring off me. I had the hallway filled with stuff, and there was plenty more to go. Needing help, I left for half an hour and returned with a couple of guys from El Salvador, their pickup truck, and some Diet Cokes. For the next few hours, I supervised as they sorted through the stuff, waited for me to say keep or go, then loaded the unwanted junk into their truck.

By late afternoon they were on their third run to wherever they took everything—I didn't ask—while I sat on a big wooden rocker, looking up at still more boxes. Not as many boxes as when we started, but more just the same.

Near the top I spotted a box different from the others. It looked interesting, so I took it down. I almost dropped it as soon as I saw the word stenciled on the side.

Mom.

• • • • •

In my hands was the box that I had been scared to open for so long. The box that I had left on counters, under tables, shunted into closets. The box that I'd stubbed my toe on, and then put into storage with everything else as a final, obvious exercise in avoidance. It was the box that contained something of my past that I was afraid to face.

It was the box that contained whatever belongings of my mom's that my sister had thought I'd want.

I picked up my knife and sliced open the cardboard.

I was no longer fearful of what I might find inside. Of what I might find out about myself.

As I peeled back the masking tape and took off the top layer of newspaper, I realized that this was what I had come

229

HELLO CRUEL WORLD

230 here for, and I didn't even know it till now.

· · · · ·

So what was inside?

Some old pillow cases, the kind my grandmother embroidered on the edge.

A cup and a saucer that my aunt had hand-painted.

And a silver tea service, which I immediately recognized as one of Mom's prize possessions.

That was it?

· · · · ·

I picked up the teapot and rubbed the side, hoping a genie would show up and grant me three wishes.

I knew what they'd be.

Bring my mom back so I could be nicer to her.

Bring my dad back so I could tell him I loved him.

Make our family a happy one.

Okay, maybe world peace. It would probably be easier than making my family happy.

· · · · ·

By this time my two helpers had returned and were looking for me to give them more work.

I put the tea set aside and removed more newspaper stuffing from my mom's box. Nothing else.

God, what a letdown. No letter. No secret note telling me what it's all about.

"Take those other boxes down," I said to my two amigos, who removed them to the truck and made their last trek.

Then I kicked the empty box marked *Mom*. It skidded to

the middle of the room and I heard something fall out. I looked. Something sparkled on the ground beside the box. I knelt down and picked it up.

I knew what it was right away.

It was a gold pin. About the size of a quarter, shaped in the form of two interlocking Ws. There were ten little diamond chips set in and around the letters, one for every ten pounds I'd lost. My old Weight Watcher's pin. My one-hundred-pound pin. I was so proud of that pin. My mom was, too. And then I'd lost it.

Or so I'd thought.

• • • • •

I flipped the diamond-encrusted Weight Watcher's pin over and over in my hand as if it were a lucky coin and thought of how right it was that I'd found it now rather than earlier. It wouldn't have been right then. Why?

Timing.

It was a message. From my mom. It had to be. There was no other explanation.

Tears filled my eyes as I realized what it was about my mom that I missed more than anything. She always believed in me. She gave me that little extra feeling of confidence and security that only comes from a mom.

That smile. That hug. That funny little look that lets you know she understands and everything is okay.

I opened my hand and looked down at the pin. It was as if I was back in Weight Watcher's. It was as if she was still here, understanding what I had been going through, searching for, and, I think, finding.

It was as if she was telling me, "You can do it, Louie. I'm **231**

232 proud of you."

I was alone. The storage room was empty of all but two or three boxes. I realized it was past dinnertime. I hadn't even noticed. Maybe for the first time in my life I didn't even care. I stuck the pin in my shirt pocket, rocked back in the chair, and said, "Thanks, Mom."

Final Reflections

3
9

Ah, the warmth of the water. The well of the past. A murky depth that makes me smile inside.

If only life was this warm and comfortable.

I wondered how long I could stay in this tub. I remembered the last time I'd felt this comfy. There was the gray cloud. Memories of skin, dust, an expanse of land that held the scent of the beginning of time.

How much time did I have now?

How much time until the hot water ran out? Could I get used to cold, soapy water? How long would it take for my skin to wrinkle like a prune? For my body to slide down the drain, into a passage I couldn't imagine?

How much time did I have?

. . . . .

I reached for the soap. The water splashed. Then the phone rang. And rang. My machine was off. I let the phone continue to ring. And ring. It became a test of wills. Whoever was calling let it ring as though they thought I lived in a five hundred-room house and had to pass through each one of them to get to the phone.

Finally, I realized it could be an emergency. Why else would somebody be so insistent on letting it ring?

I rose from the tub, dripping water and soap, like a monster from some nightmare of an Ivory commercial—the Soap Thing. Naturally, though, as soon as I put both feet on the floor, the phone stopped ringing.

"Gawwwwwdaaaaaamit!"

Now I faced a choice: returning to the safety and comfort of the tub or entering the cold, cruel world. I stood motionless. Dripping. Listening to the dripping of water and soap. I turned my head and saw myself in the mirror.

. . . . .

You know, even when you're alone, I realized, you're never really alone. There's always yourself to contend with.

. . . . .

I looked long and deeply at myself. I started at the top of my head. My hair. Then my face. My eyes. Down to my neck. Then I canvassed by big body. My shoulders didn't look fat.

My chest was okay, not great, but better. My arms still held too much fat, loose skin that was like unwanted hangers-on. But also not as much as before. My stomach was next.

Only twice the size it should've been. Which was smaller. It used to be three times too big. I could actually see the beginnings of a waist.

Then onto my legs. Soft tree trunks. They were strong. From what I could see, they were used to carrying this load. My knees were well-defined, calves hard as a rock, the ankles of a thin person, and feet that belonged to a dancer. Feet that were fast, that had places to go.

I looked back up at my eyes. Into my eyes. They were also strong, and determined, full of wonder, curiosity, sensitivity —and love. I hadn't been able to see that too clearly before, but I saw it now.

I realized that this was me. All of me.

The naked truth.

And it wasn't bad. In fact, it was good. Darn good.

Why hadn't I seen this before? Thank God I could see it now.

If this turned out to be me forever, I thought, then okay, fine. I'll go with it.

I'll even love it.

• • • • •

The phone started ringing again. This time I didn't wait. I picked it up.

"Hello?"

"Hi," the voice said. "This is Susan from Clinton-Gore headquarters. Do you know who you're voting for?"

"Yes," I answered. "But first I have to tell you something." **235**

H E L L O C R U E L W O R L D

236   "Yes?"

"I'm naked," I said. "I'm fat and I'm naked, and I think that's just fine."

Being a true enthusiastic volunteer, she replied in a sunny voice, "That's great! Do you plan on voting Democratic?"

"No," I said. There was a pause.

"Well, who are you voting for?" she asked.

I thought for a moment.

"Did you call before and let the phone ring?" I asked.

"Maybe," she said. "I don't remember. Probably. I mean, if you're on my list . . ."

"I'm voting for Nixon," I said, laughing, and then I hung up the phone.

Still butt naked as the day I was born, I walked over to the living room window, opened it, felt the sun against my skin, leaned out and yelled at the top of my lungs, "I love you, Louie Anderson."

For the first time in a long time, maybe for the first time in my life, I had no problem imagining that somebody, somewhere, heard me and yelled back, "I love you, too."

It felt good.